T0361167

SOCIAL DEVELOPMENT IN KERALA: ILLUSION
OR REALITY?

This book is dedicated to people all over the world who imagine and reimagine development.

Social Development in Kerala: Illusion or Reality?

SUNDAR RAMANATHAIYER
Edith Cowan University, Western Australia
STEWART MACPHERSON
City University of Hong Kong

Routledge
Taylor & Francis Group
LONDON AND NEW YORK

First published 2000 by Ashgate Publishing

Reissued 2018 by Routledge
2 Park Square, Milton Park, Abingdon, Oxon OX14 4RN
711 Third Avenue, New York, NY 10017, USA

Routledge is an imprint of the Taylor & Francis Group, an informa business

Publisher's Note
The publisher has gone to great lengths to ensure the quality of this reprint but points out that some imperfections in the original copies may be apparent.

Disclaimer
The publisher has made every effort to trace copyright holders and welcomes correspondence from those they have been unable to contact.

A Library of Congress record exists under LC control number: 00132610

ISBN 13: 978-1-138-71575-2 (hbk)
ISBN 13: 978-1-315-19739-5 (ebk)

Contents

List of Figures

List of Tables

List of Contributors

*Sundar **Ramanathaiyer*** was born and brought up in Kerala. He has been writing in Malayalam and English on social development in Kerala and development perspectives of Indian cartoonists. Sundar has translated Aubrey Menen's autobiographical fiction 'The Space Within The Heart' to Malayalam, published short stories and associated in film making. He is currently pursuing PhD in development studies at Edith Cowan University, Western Australia.

*Professor Stewart **MacPherson*** was born in the UK and has taught at universities in UK, Uganda, Tanzania, Papua New Guinea and Hong Kong. He has written and edited a number of books on social welfare, social development and social administration. Stewart is currently a Professor associated with Edith Cowan University, Western Australia and City University of Hong Kong. He is now an Australian citizen developing an olive farm in the far South West of Australia.

Preface

The authors of this book dare to doubt, question, and critique what has become accepted knowledge. Sri Lanka and Kerala have created cult following in the "development circle". "Development as a practical and intellectual project has been steeped in optimism" (Tucker, 1999: 1) yet there have been few successful examples after decades of development, many places are in more debilitated conditions than previously. Sri Lanka has been a high achiever in social development. With low economic growth, significant progress has been made in human development indicators (literacy, life expectancy, and infant mortality). There has however, for the past fifteen years, been a civil and conflict war between the government and the Liberation Tigers of Tamil Ealam (LTTE) with severe abuses of human life suffered. More than 16,000 people have 'disappeared', upto 10 % of the population has been displaced from their homes and thousands have been killed. Human rights abuses continue to be perpetuated by both military and separatists. The vast majority of human rights violation (torture, rape, individual killings, illegal and arbitrary detention) remain unresolved. Shortage of food and supplies continue in areas of conflict (Human Rights Watch 1999 World Report). When 'development' is considered in the broad context, can a place that has been enduring continual civil war become a model of successful development? As this book goes to press, reports from Kerala indicate that in the past week (December 1999), senseless killings of people in the northern region continue to occur in the name of politics and religion, and Kerala remains in a state of fear and paralysis.

Kerala still remains an example of social development that works. Movies, documentaries, articles, researchers, aid workers, governmental officials all pay homage to the successes of Kerala, a place of low productivity and economic growth, of extreme population pressures and of unbelievable human development gains. In spite of a large population and despite decades of low income and low-productivity growth, Kerala has made human development gains that are greater than those of other Indian states and of many developing nations. Kerala's Human Development Index (HDI) ranks it higher than all other Indian states and more than 20 places higher than India (UNDP, 1996: 81). The keys to this success have been attributed to good nutrition based on an efficient public food distribution system; a strong and consistent political commitment to public education; and matrilineal social structures and a lack of social opposition to women's education and social economic advancement (Dreze & Sen, 1995).

Good health, adequate nutrition, literacy, and employment need to be treated as essential human rights, just as they were in 1948 when the international community adopted the Universal Declarations of Human Rights. In the new millennium, the eradication of extreme poverty still remains the biggest problem to address by the world's nations. More people live today in a condition of poverty than at any other time in the history of the world. Yet, this is a time of extreme wealth for a few, of unprecedented technical ability, a time of computer information highways, trade summitry and material prosperity. The ever widening gap between extreme deprivation and extreme wealth is obscene. No person deserves to live in abject poverty and each individual deserves the right to live with dignity. As human species we have the ability to imagine, to dream of social justice and harmony.

But the reality is that economic and social development is often painful, cruel and uneven. Divisions between wealthy and poor, between male and female, between oppressor and oppressed exist within countries as they do between countries. The past simplistic notion of East and West, North and South, rich and poor to describe nations denies the complexity of life and human existence in the late twentieth century. Rajini Kothari (1993: 146) proposes the "phenomenon of the two Indias". One India is progressing rapidly creating new technologies, information, and resources. The other India is impoverished, malnourished, toiling continually to survive. These people have little access to resources and while serving the wealthy India through their daily toil have little or no say in how the country is run, where resources are used, or how their lives are governed. India like other nations has entered the new millennium to face the continued social injustice. The great poverty of millions Indians is not a poverty of resources, rather it is a poverty of justice. Despite half a century of government commitment to alleviating poverty through legislative and policy measures, India remains a divided country, a country of the rich and a country inhabited by the very poor. Among the most painful manifestations of social injustice in India is this persistence of abject poverty of a great number of people.

International attention has been focussed on poverty eradication for decades. The United Nations Development Programme's (UNDP) 1998 report entitled, *Overcoming Human Poverty* shows that people and groups including aid organizations, governments and development agencies are committed to the goals set by the World Summit for Social Development in 1995. The eradication of poverty continues to be and will be the mission of the UNDP. The *Copenhagen Plus Five* of the Social Summit at the United Nations to be held in the year 2000 will publish the results of social development efforts for each country. Individuals, governments and non-governmental organizations worldwide, will be questioned as to the progress in addressing poverty, unemployment and social integration, the goals of the Social Summit (UNRISD, 1997). Meanwhile, for a majority of people who are poor, unemployed and often in fear, progress simply means surviving yet another day.

There are limitless numbers of pages written by authors who analyse why poverty still exists, why development has not occurred equally to all people, why millions of people continue to be trapped within worlds of hunger, illiteracy, poverty. These authors often obfuscate the reality of life for individual people, women, men, and children by discussing "development" as somehow separate from people. But as Arturo Escobar (1995) argues the peoples of Asia, Africa and Latin America never saw themselves in terms of "development". They are involved in a day to day struggle to survive. The reality remains that the rich have gotten richer and the poor have become relatively poorer despite the many theories of development and the programmes devoted to poverty alleviation.

Kerala is often cited as an example of people-targeted development, which has been achieved through measures different than those usually recommended by Northern countries or development specialists. Kerala's status as development has been attributed to social development with low economic growth through people oriented programmes. Analyst Govinda Parayil (quoted in Bissio, 1999: 76) explains that Kerala was able to eliminate acute poverty, without "a swift growth of its per capita GDP, as expected of all models and theories of economic development". The success of Kerala has been attributed to a broad nexus of factors including social movements, citizen participation, land reform, literacy, especially among women, and free primary education for all.

Sundar Ramanathaiyer from Kerala and Stewart MacPherson from Australia seek to unravel the relationship between dimensions of social and economic development in Kerala. They propose that only a balanced socio-economic approach leads to true development and they search beyond the rhetoric to uncover the reality of Kerala's development experience. What are the development realities and development illusions? This book is exciting for the authors begin to doubt and through a meticulous process of research expose a raw, comprehensive, and complex picture of Kerala. Socio-economic data is analyzed at the panchayat district level, to encompass low (Krishnapuram, in a district famous for workers' movements), mid (Andoorkonam, in the capital of Kerala), and high (Karoor, part of a district famous for cash crops and popular magazines) geographical regions. Data from the more than 10,000 households surveyed in these districts is publicly released for the first time. This study reveals the levels and geographic distribution of those living in poverty or affluence. The authors seek more than statistical data to understand how people live, in what surroundings and under what conditions. Included is crucial information on the previously oppressed classes - the scheduled castes and tribes.

Ramanathaiyer visited the back lanes and alleys, meeting with "visibly poor" elderly men, women and children, speaking with them, and listening to their stories. He found that women were most articulate in explaining what they have, do not have, and need in order to live better. Through this, the authors paint a comprehensive picture of Kerala. We learn how people live from day to day, in what kind of house, located where, how women cook and on what type of stove, where water is collected and waste disposed of, what possessions do people own or want to own - bicycles, jeeps, radios, televisions.

Officials, all of whom had at least ten years experience in the state government of Kerala, were interviewed in depth to determine their understanding of the nature and quality of social welfare programmes and the difficulties they face in implementing these programmes. The frustrations of these officials reflect the paradoxes of the 'Kerala Model of Development'. Their views are supplemented with the statistical data concerning the levels of spending on social welfare programmes.

In this book, life in Kerala is described, not from one perspective but from several. People live in the same state but obviously share very different realities, often not inter-connecting or seeing each other worlds, divided by class, gender, wealth, occupation. For example in Karoor, the high level panchayat, "The Indian Coffee House in Palai is crowded with affluent youth. On the sides of the road are beggars, blind and lame, waiting for the mercy of passers-by, who are oblivious to their presence".

Gender relations and the equality of opportunity for both men and women are central to any analysis of development. While the indicators show that women in Kerala are 'better off', the following observation describes day to day lived reality of Kerala women. "Once inside a crowded bus, you cannot help noticing that the seats reserved for women are occupied by men. This is nothing unusual-all over Kerala, we encounter the same situation". Women with small babies are ignored as men take the seats on buses seemingly oblivious to the need of women balancing packages and children while standing on crowded buses. This is a book about the dignity of life, revealing people, place and time. We are led through the labyrinth of smells, scenery, and sounds to meet the residents.

The authors suggest that while 'models' and 'theories of development' are useful for simplifying issues, women, men, and children live much more complex and dynamic lives than any theory or indicators would suggest. Never do Ramanathaiyer and McPherson lose sight of the people in development, the reason for citizen participation, policies, and governmental programmes. They ask fundamental questions concerning the development experience in Kerala upheld as a 'model of development'. They question whether continued gains in social development can occur without substantial economic development experienced by a broad range of people in Kerala and not only the male elite. The authors also suggest that the development experience in Kerala has not been a result of democratic participation from all levels of society but rather demonstrate that a top-down, bureaucratic approach has been perpetuated. Based on their comprehensive research, they conclude that "any society that is insensitive and indifferent to the primary needs the people does not deserve to be called socially developed, much less a 'model' for the rest of the world".

References

Bissio, R., 1999 (ed), *The World Guide: An Alternative Reference to the Countries of our Planet 1999/2000*, Montevideo: Instituto del Tercer Mundo.

Dreze, J. and A. Sen, 1995, *India: Economic Development and Social Opportunity*, Oxford and Delhi: Oxford University Press.

Escobar, A., 1995, 'Imagining a post-development era', in J. Crush (ed.) *Power of Development*, London & New York: Routledge, pp. 211-28.

Kothari, R., 1993, *Growing Amnesia: An Essay on Poverty and the Human Consciousness*, New Delhi: Viking Press.

Tucker, V., 1999, 'The myth of development: A critique of a Eurocentric discourse', in R. Munck and D. O'Hearn (eds), *Critical Development Theory*, London: Zed Books, pp 1-27.

United Nations Development Programme (UNDP) 1996, New York: UNDP.

United Nations Development Programme (UNDP) 1998, *Overcoming Human Poverty*, New York: UN.

United Nations Research Institute for Social Development (UNRISD), 1997, *Advancing the Social Agenda: Two Years After Copenhagen*, Geneva: UNRISD.

Nancy Hudson-Rodd,
Edith Cowan University,
Western Australia.

Acknowledgements

We wish to express our sincere gratitude to the many people who made this book possible. Our sense of indebtedness is especially great to the people of Krishnapuram, Andoorkonam and Karoor, Kerala. Our gratitude to the Director and other officials of Centre for Earth Sciences Studies, Thiruvananthapuram, for providing valuable socio-economic data, and to the eight senior government officials of Kerala, who spent hours sharing their insights on Kerala development experience. We are also thankful to the officials of several departments in Kerala, who provided us with secondary data on Kerala.

Our thanks goes to several friends, including T.K. Sadasivan, S. Sam, V. Sasi, Sreevasudeva Bhattathiri who helped us unravel and understand the grass-root realities of Kerala. We also have immensely benefited from the discussions with Dr. Laurie Baker, Prof. Gopalakrishnan Nair, Dr. Govindan Parayil, Dr. Ramesh Kini, Dr.V. Rajagopal, Dr. Soman, Prof. Wesley Shrum, Pramod Menon, T.T. Sreekumar, N.R.S. Babu, K.P. Vijayan and P. Sujathan.

We cannot thank Prof. Veronica Pearson enough for her inspiring support and critical comments on the earlier drafts of this book. And of course without the support of Girija Krishnaswamy and Sarah MacPherson, this book would have remained a dream.

No statement of indebtedness would be complete without mentioning those who have imagined and reimagined Kerala development. We also thank in advance those who would endorse and challenge our findings.

Finally, we do apologize to our dear children - Ramanathan and Megan - who missed a lot of attention in our encounter with illusions and realities of social development in Kerala.

1 Kerala – Behind the Illusions and Realities

For the past two decades, the south Indian state of Kerala (pronounced Ker'uh luh), often hailed as a 'model of development', has attracted much academic and media attention. The response to an international congress on Kerala studies (August 27–29, 1994) under the auspices of A.K.G. Centre for Research and Studies, Thiruvananthapuram, Kerala, was overwhelming. Around 1,600 persons, of whom nearly 700 were academics, attended the congress. There were participants from 23 countries other than India. The series of articles and responses on Kerala development debate by scholars from several countries in the Bulletin of Concerned Asian Scholars (January-March, 1998, July-September 1998, October-December, 1998) exemplify the continued interest in Kerala development experience.

These are not isolated examples. British Broadcasting Corporation (1992) telecast a documentary on Kerala's development achievements. Canadian Broadcasting Corporation (1988) and the Netherlands Television Trust for the Environment (1990) produced programmes on fertility decline in Kerala. *Monthly Review* (1991) dedicated an entire issue for debate on Kerala development. *The New Internationalist* (1993) came out with a special issue on Kerala's development experience. *Human Development Report* (1993 and 1996) referred to the positive disparity in Kerala's human development achievements. The Institute for Food and Development Policy promotes Kerala for eco-tourism. Internet sites have home pages on Kerala development and for a Kerala bibliography. Students of development visit Kerala to study the 'mystery of Kerala'.

The past

During 19th century and to a great extent, the first two decades of the 20th century, Kerala was an extremely caste-ridden society. *Jati* (birth) not only determined the occupations, but also the level of participation of individuals in society. The caste system determined the dress code, type of housing and freedom of movement. The lower castes were not permitted to live in tiled houses, move in conveyances, or even use metallic vessels. Women of lower castes were not permitted to wear blouses or cover their breasts. Public roads were not accessible to lower castes and the permissible social and geographical distance between the upper and lower castes was clearly outlined.

Jati system denied the lower castes the right of entry into temples. They were not allowed to bathe in the temple ponds. They did not have the right to draw water from wells belonging to upper castes. They could never dream of holding an umbrella even during the monsoon seasons. All along, all throughout the year, they had to use self-debasing forms of speech, while communicating with the people of upper castes. Untouchability was the norm of Kerala society. The caste system was so rigorous and primitive, that it prompted the Hindu reformer Swami Vivekananda to call Kerala, 'a mad house of caste'.

The transformation

The socio-religious movements since the dawn of the 20th century have transformed the socio-cultural landscape of Kerala. Today, in Kerala, unlike several other parts of India, caste does not determine the level of education and the type of occupation. The previously oppressed classes participate in all walks of society. Their rights are not denied. Social mobility is no more a dream for them. This aspect of Kerala society is very significant because in several other Indian states, the previously oppressed castes still have to fight for basic human dignity. *Time* (25 March 1996) reported a strike by the agricultural labourers of the central Indian village of Ekwari. These labourers who belong to the *dalits*, literally meaning broken people, demanded the right to sit (and not squat) when they receive instructions from their upper caste landlords, and also the right to wear wrist watches. Keralites would be shocked to read this.

The depressing and agonizing scenes of child workers in hazardous environments are totally absent in Kerala. Female infanticide, still prevalent in several other states, is unheard of here. Irrespective of caste, class and gender, children attend schools. Child marriage, still a social problem in several other Indian states, is not common in Kerala. Most important, any sort of caste discrimination, is a tale of the past.

A land cherishing a legend

In the collective consciousness of Kerala is the myth of king *Mahabali*, during whose reign, all human beings were equal, and there were no lies and no deceit. The legend describes how Gods, jealous of the reign of Mahabali, tricked him to the underworld, but had to grant him the boon of being able to visit his beloved subjects once a year. Thus every year, during *Onam*, the national festival of Kerala, all Keralites, irrespective of caste, creed or religion, welcome the 'annual visit' of Mahabali. They cherish the poetic memories of a bygone era – a period of equity and equality. In effect, the dreams of an egalitarian society find their finer expressions in celebrating Onam during the most beautiful season of the year.

We can understand contemporary Kerala only when we put Kerala in perspective by comparing it with other Indian states.. We would have to plot Kerala in the larger canvas of Indian reality, or for that matter third world reality, in order to realize how much Kerala differs from other regions.

Kerala – an overview

Kerala is one of the 25 states in India. It has an area of 38,863 sq.km, occupying 1.18 per cent of the Indian Union and a population of 29 million (*Census of India*, 1991). The state of Kerala came into existence on 1 November 1956, as a result of the State Re-organization Act 1956. A greater part of Travancore, Cochin and Malabar were united to form the state of Kerala. It has the Arabian sea on the west and the Western Ghats (mountains) in the east. The territory is divided into low land (less than 7.6 m. below sea level), mid-land (7.6 to 76 m. above sea level); and highland (76 m. above sea level) regions. The sandy strip of low-land, covering 10 per cent of the geographical area, is characterized by numerous backwaters. Paddy and coconuts are cultivated here. In the mid-levels, with 42 per cent of the geographical area, paddy, tapioca, spices, plantain, etc., are cultivated. The highland, with 48 per cent of the geographical area, is mountainous in nature, with forests in the upper range and plantation crops in the lower range. Twenty-six per cent of the population lives in the lowland, 59 per cent in the midland, and 15 per cent in highland regions. Density of population is highest in lowland (1,385 per sq.km.) and lowest in highland (172 per sq.km.). In the midland region, the density of population is 778 per sq.km.

The climate is semi-tropical, hot and moist, with temperatures ranging from 80 degree F to 90 degree F. Kerala gets an annual rainfall which varies from 1,250 mm to 5,000 mm with an average of 3,085 mm.

Administratively, Kerala is divided into 14 districts, 63 Taluks, 152 community development blocks and 991 gram panchayats. The settlement pattern in Kerala is different from other Indian states, in the sense that Kerala does not have a village system with a common node. It is difficult to differentiate one village from another (Sreekumar, 1993).

The state is generally classified as 'backward' in terms of its poor industrial development and faltering production of foodgrains.

What is written above is an overall macro picture of Kerala society and is intended as a curtain raiser. What follows is the debate about the relationship between social and economic aspects of development; description of the theoretical framework, research questions and methodology of the study.

Economic and social aspects of development

The relationship between economic development and social development is complex. There are four major possible combinations of this relationship (Table 1.1).

Developed countries could be broadly classified as falling into the first category. The low-income countries of the third world are neither economically nor socially developed. In Arabian countries, the disparity between economic development and social development is very high. They have failed in transforming their economic gains to social development. Sri

Lanka and Kerala are cited to be examples of having achieved high social development at low economic growth (Franke and Chasin, 1994).

Table 1.1   Possible relationships between economic and social development

High economic development and High social development

Low economic development and Low social development

High economic development and Low social development

Low economic development and High social development

Essentially there are two major streams in development theory, dealing with the relationship between economic and social components of development. First is the classical 'trickle–down' theory, in which it is assumed that the benefits of economic development will 'trickle–down' to the masses. 'This perspective suggests that economic growth is both a *necessary and sufficient condition* for the improvement of the lives of the majority of the population in a society' (MacPherson, 1996, p. 1). It has been proved beyond doubt that economic growth is not a sufficient condition for social development (Seers, 1969, MacPherson, 1995). The disillusionment with the growth theories led to the evolution of the 'trickle–up' hypothesis which emphasized the satisfaction of basic human needs like health and education (Streeten, 1972, 1981). Broadly, the theoretical framework of development could be classified into social development as a product of economic growth and economic growth as a result of social development (Newman and Thomson, 1989). The approaches are diagrammatically represented in Figure 1.1.

In reality, it is very difficult to simply categorize development experience as economic or social. For example, starting an educational institution is both an economic and social development activity. The construction of buildings provides employment to people, the institution needs teaching and non-teaching faculty, which again is an employment generating activity. When an educational institution is started, the area tends to 'develop' with more shops and residences. On the other hand, by imparting a set of useful skills and capabilities to its students, the institution catalyzes further personal, social and economic development of the region. Another simple example is that of a kitchen garden – it is both an economic and ecological activity. Even while the vegetables are for domestic consumption and not sold in the neighbourhood market, the family saves money they otherwise would have spent on vegetables. Vegetable gardening is an eco-friendly activity because, though in a small way, it questions the entire network of production and marketing, raises people from the state of dependency, and breaks the chains of core and periphery.

Figure 1.1   Approaches to development

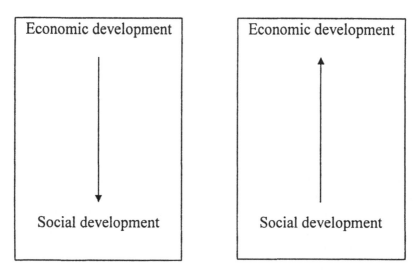

The most difficult problem in assessing the relationship between economic development and social development is establishing causality. Some researchers (Ram, 1979; Hicks, 1980) have established that social development at a given level would increase the chances of further economic development at a later stage, rather than the other way round.

The causal priority question can be as tricky as the eternal chicken or egg puzzle.

There have been numerous studies of development in Kerala examining the relationship between social and economic development. Franke and Chasin (1990) argue that the radical reforms in Kerala indicate that economic growth is not a prerequisite for progress. They argue that the redistribution policies of the Kerala government have resulted in improvement of the quality of life. In another study of Nadur village in Kerala, Franke (1993) establishes that life in Kerala *is a little better*.[1] Panikar and Soman (1984) and Kannan et. al (1991) have done studies on health; Zachariah et. al (1994) on demographic transition; Jeffrey (1992) and Saradamoni (1994) on women in Kerala;. George, P.S. (1979) and. Kumar, S.K. (1979) on the public distribution system in Kerala; and Ramachandran, V.K. (1995) on development achievements. George, K.K. (1990, 1993) has done extensive studies on the fiscal crisis of Kerala and on the limitations of the Kerala model of development.

Theoretical framework of the study

The model proposed here has its origin in Chinese philosophy. The concepts of *yin* and *yang* have been adopted to denote the economic and social aspects of development. The argument is that both are essential for 'true development' (Figure 1.2).

Figure 1.2 Harmony between social and economic development

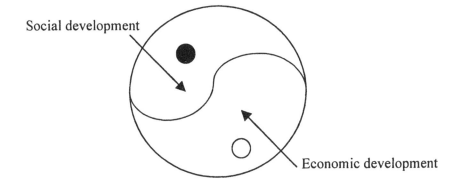

True development is the freedom from the diseases of poverty, illiteracy and unemployment. Irrespective of class, caste or gender, true development empowers women, eradicates contagious diseases, ensures food and nutrition, and provides health care to all sections of people. True development guarantees expression of individual freedom in politics and society. All these may seem like rhetoric, wishful thinking of a utopia. Still –

Without resources, no nation can invest in social development and without high quality human resources (a by-product of social development), no nation can economically develop (unless the country has rich natural resources, which are neither infinite nor, due to inherent inequalities in the distribution of resources, capable of automatically ensuring development for the majority of people) and reduce inequality in society. The social inputs like provision of education and health care are extremely important in the overall development of a nation. These social inputs require economic inputs and without a fair amount of growth, however egalitarian the philosophy of a nation is, the efforts directed at social development are unsustainable. In other words, for attaining 'true development', the economic and social aspects of development are to be complementary in nature. Thus the model suggests that the socio-economic dimensions are highly interactive, complementary. and interdependent. This model assumes that harmony between economic and social development is essential. Only a balanced socio-economic development will lead to true development. The absence of one will pull the other down, affecting the harmony. Economic development without social development is meaningless and social development without economic development will be at the cost of quality and is not sustainable. Economic development by itself will not result in social development and social development need not result in economic development.

The study

The overall objective of the study is to find out whether the 'Kerala model' of development is as good as that is claimed to be. In other words, to find out whether social development in Kerala is a reality or an illusion. To separate illusions from realities, the following specific objectives are charted out.

1. Since the Kerala model of development, in a broad sense, could be defined as high social development at low economic growth, a major objective of the study is to assess the relationship between economic development and social development in the Kerala context.
2. To analyze the context, nature and content of social policies and welfare programmes formulated and implemented in Kerala as distinct from the other Indian states and evaluate their achievements, and
3. To assess the role and contribution of state government in the social development process of Kerala.

Steps in the research process

The four major steps in data collection are given in Table 1.2.

Table 1.2   Steps in data collection

1	2	3	4
Identifying and collecting secondary data on macro-level socio-economic aspects of Kerala and other Indian states	Identifying the micro-level socio-economic data.	Identifying and interviewing the development officials in various government departments	Visiting the panchayats under study

In Kerala, most often, nothing works without contacts. Even with the right contacts, one has to be consistently efficient to 'get things done'. Despite the personal contacts built up over the last two decades by Ramanathaiyer, we found the data collection tiring. On the one hand, identifying the sources of secondary data on macro-level socio-economic realities of Kerala and other Indian states was a difficult task. The very framework of enquiry, which covers several social and economic aspects of Kerala society, made the identification and collection of data unwieldy. We had to rely on government officials for secondary data. Lack of facilities like proper transportation or photocopying machines was a major hurdle. The most frustrating moments in the government offices were when 'the person concerned was on leave'. In such situations other officials, who were willing to help found themselves helpless – the records are in the 'personal custody' of some official. The most shocking incident was when an official in the Public Relations Department refused to give any previous publications on the ground that 'with every change in the Ministry, we treat the previous publications as obsolete'. On probing further, he said that the there were instances of officials being reprimanded by politicians for issuing documents on the previous ministries. The irony was that he even refused to give the publications brought out during the period of rule by a different faction of the same political party. Despite the various difficulties, fortunately, it was possible for us to collect extensive data on several socio-economic aspects of Kerala society.

Methodology

The methodology adopted in this research is different from the previous studies on Kerala. This study attempts to look at both the macro and micro-level realities of social development in Kerala. Secondary data on the socio-economic aspects of Kerala's development, along with survey data on the standard of living of families in three different geographical levels of Kerala are also analyzed. The methodology of the study is described below.

Macro-level

1. *Analysis of secondary data*
    1. To compare the development aspects of Kerala with other Indian states.
    2. To understand the socio-economic condition of Kerala; to see whether Kerala has achieved higher social development in relation to its economic development.
    3. To evaluate the 'Kerala model' of development.
    4. To assess the role and contribution of state government towards social development in Kerala and to evaluate the social sector expenditure of Kerala in comparison with other Indian states.
2. *Interview method*
    5. To understand the perceptions of development officials on development processes in Kerala.
    6. To identify the approaches to development in Kerala.

7. To find out the impact of economic reforms on social development in Kerala and to understand the future directions.

Micro level

1. *Analysis of socio-economic data of three panchayats in Kerala*
   1. To study the socio-economic condition of the population, treating households as units.
   2. To evaluate the inter-regional differences.
   3. To find out the level of poverty/affluence of the households; to compare the living standards of the 'previously oppressed classes' with the general population.
2. *Ethnographic research*
   4. To study, compare and contrast the living conditions of different classes of people in the panchayats under study, through observation and informal communication.

Socio-economic data from secondary sources on major Indian states, particularly on Kerala, was collected. This data were analyzed using regression to explore the relationship between economic development and social development.

Data on social spending in major Indian states were collected and analyzed to see whether Kerala had been spending more on social sectors than other Indian states.

Materials from the in-depth interviews with Kerala state government officials supplement this analysis. Eight officials were interviewed by Ramanathaiyer about their perceptions on development, the nature and quality of social welfare programmes in Kerala and the difficulties they face in implementing these programmes. It was not easy to identify the officials and get them to 'open up'. Since the area of study is vast and not limited to a couple of areas of administration, several officials from various departments were contacted. The selection of officials was based on their experience in development departments. All the interviewees have worked for a minimum of a decade in Kerala government service. Despite the fact that secondary data are not available for fisherfolk, an in-depth interview with a senior fisheries development official shed light on the development and deprivation of Kerala fisherfolk.

The main methodology is the analysis of socio-economic data at the panchayat level. This data were collected by Centre for Earth Science Studies (CESS) in the year 1992 as part of the panchayat resource mapping programme. CESS collected data on resources and socio-economic conditions of Kerala at panchayat level with people's participation, to help decentralized planning. Three panchayats, representing the low, mid and high geographical regions of Kerala were selected for use in this study. These are: *Krishnapuram* in Alappuzha district (the district famous for workers' movements), representing the low levels; *Andoorkonam* in Thiruvananthapuram district (the capital of Kerala and the erstwhile princely state of Travancore), representing the mid levels; and *Karoor* in Kottayam district (the district famous for cash crops and centre for popular magazines), representing the high levels.

The survey had generated data on 3,389 households in the low-level panchayat, 3,503 households in the mid-level panchayat and 3,792 households in the high-level panchayat Thus altogether, data have been generated for 10,684 households.[2] This is the first time these data have been used outside government circles.

The available data set had both advantages and disadvantages. That the data were collected for the population as a whole, is a major advantage. It is worth mentioning that it would have been impossible for the authors to conduct a survey of the scale and depth of the resource mapping data.

One limitation of the sample is that it does not include a coastal panchayat or a tribal panchayat. Recent studies of the Kerala development experience treat both fisherfolk and tribals as 'outliers', implying that these sections of the society are still marginalized and have not yet benefited much from the development pursuits of Kerala society. This by no means belittles the scope of the data available.

On going through the ward-wise data, it was found that the quality of housing and sanitation in some wards were worse than in other wards, and that it was possible that poor people would be concentrated more in some wards. During visits to the panchayats it was confirmed that wards nearer to junctions and main roads had more middle-class and rich people, while wards further away from the main roads and junctions had a greater proportion of people who were poor. This prevented the adoption of any sampling method, for fear of losing the true picture. Hence the entire data set is used in the analysis.

By ascribing scores for facilities and possessions, an attempt has been made to bring out a poverty/affluence level of the panchayats under study. Apart from understanding the poverty profile of the total population, this analysis has also helped in understanding the standards of living of the previously oppressed classes (the scheduled castes and scheduled tribes), in relation to the general population. Though no panchayats in the sample are tribal panchayats, the population of scheduled tribes in the data available exceeds the state average. In other words, the state of scheduled tribes in the mainstream population is available, while the state of tribals in exclusion, is absent. Individual data of the mid-level panchayat (Andoorkonam) for 16,865 household members have been compiled and used for analyzing the demographic characteristics, viz., marital status, literacy levels and educational attainments of the population in the mid-level panchayat.

Brief sketches of the panchayats supplement the analysis. Ramanathaiyer visited these panchayats in July 1996, travelled extensively and verified the available data at random. He walked into the lanes and bylanes of these panchayats and met people – mostly the elderly, women and children. People, especially women and children, who were visibly poor, were most welcoming and talked in-depth about their problems. Being sure of what they have and do not have and what they wanted, women articulated their demands well.

Scheme of the book

The book consists of six chapters. It begins with the description of the research problem and the methodology used. The second chapter is a discussion of the achievements, failures and paradoxes of the Kerala model of development and statistical analysis of the economic development-social development disparity in Kerala. In Chapter three, after discussing the role of government in social sectors, the statistical significance of governmental expenditure on social sectors (whether above or below that which is expected of its gross domestic product) is analyzed. Chapter four, based on extensive interviews with senior state government officials, describe their perceptions on social development processes in Kerala, the approaches to development, the impact of economic reforms and the future of social development in Kerala. Chapter five looks deep into the micro-level realities of Kerala society, by analyzing the facilities (housing, cooking methods and fuel used, source of drinking water, sanitation etc.) and possessions (moveable and immovable, like radio, television, and cycle, jeep etc.) of 10,684 families in the three different geographical levels of Kerala. The incidence of poverty and affluence of the households are also analyzed, by arriving at aggregate scores for the households, on the basis of individual scores assigned to each of the facilities and possessions The socio-economic data of 16,865 household members of mid-level panchayat are also analyzed in this chapter. Chapter six, the concluding chapter, describes the realities and illusions of social development in Kerala.

Notes

1   *Life is a little better: Redistribution as a Development Strategy in Nadur Village Kerala*, is the title of Franke's book on Nadur village in Kerala.
2   The sheer volume of the data posed enormous problems in processing. Details of the various steps involved in data processing and analysis are given in Chapter 5.

2 Achievements and Failures of Kerala Model of Development

The genesis of the 'Kerala model of development', a term, widely used in development literature is unknown. Raj (1995), who, with his colleagues at the Centre for Development Studies (CDS), Thiruvananthapuram, Kerala, prepared the pioneer study on Kerala development,[1] states that the Centre has at 'no stage described its findings on the set of issues as constituting in effect a "Kerala model"' (p. 12).

Isaac and Tharakan (1995) report that the term Kerala model was mentioned in the same international congress 'in a bewildering variety of notions, some in explicitly normative terms' (p. 1993). The term Kerala model might have originated out of Kerala's development experience in attaining high scores on physical qualities of life indices at low per capita income. Though another coining 'Kerala–Sri Lanka model' (Timberg, 1981) did not catch on, it reflects the similarities in the development patterns of Kerala and Sri Lanka.

The Kerala model of development has been termed a 'social justice model' (Franke, 1995), an 'enigma' (McKibben, 1996), an exemplar of the 'basic needs approach' (Hellar, 1995), etc. Though Sen (1994) does not use the term 'model', he says: 'Despite the fact that economic growth of Kerala has been sluggish ... it has been able to achieve tremendous results in important areas such as literacy, life expectancy and mortality rates. The Indian government *should try to emulate* the Kerala experience' (emphasis added; cited in Vijayanand 1995, p. 1). McKibben (1995) goes one step further and remarks that Kerala could be as significant a schoolhouse for the rich world as for the poor.

At the same time, others disagree. To Namboodiripad (1995), the leader of CPI (M), who incidentally was heading the party in introducing land reforms and providing several social security measures, the Kerala model, is 'one of deindustrialization', a created fable that:

15

a country or state can prosper without industrialization, without the modernized development of agriculture, the development of modern secular and scientific education and culture etc. invented by the apologists of the imperialistic policy of deindustrialization and backwardness of our state (*The Hindu*, 11 September 1995, p. 5).

Though belonging to the opposite camp and though not so sharp in criticizing the 'model', Antony (1995), leader of the Congress Party and ex-Chief Minister of the state believes that the Kerala model neglected productive aspects.

In a cautious evaluation, Nair (1995), another ex-Chief Minister and leader of the Communist Party of India observed that:

> the Kerala model cannot altogether be dismissed as a good for nothing pattern of development. It has certainly helped the state go forward. However, lack of follow up actions might even destroy the gains made by it (*The Hindu*, 18 September 1995; p. 5).

Saradamoni (1994) is of the opinion that Kerala has not become a development model, but has uncritically accepted and internalized other models. She questions the Kerala model of development in which 'diversity has no place'. She believes that the values of world systems introduced in Kerala, through developmental programmes, administration, education and media, have created a false sense of security. She argues that every solution in Kerala created new problems, and no attempt to understand and solve the issues in totality was made.

> Education and educated unemployed, land reform legislation which did not include production, productivity or employment in its agenda, political awareness or group rights without the essential sense of responsibility both at individual and collective levels are just few examples in this context (p. 508).[2]

Quoting the often cited examples of Sri Lanka and Kerala, Martin (1979), former Chairman of the Organisation for Economic Co-operation and Development's (OECD) Development Assistance Committee questions the PQLI test of progress. Admitting that Sri Lanka and Kerala 'have shown that it is not too hard to achieve a reasonably good PQLI with scant resources', he questions the 'over commitment to panaceas', which fails to generate employment and income (p. 18). From the premise that a 'longer life need not be a better one', he argues that PQLI path of development leads only to a dead end.

Before discussing the Kerala model further, let us see how Kerala fares in social and economic development parameters in a comparative setting. The Kerala development pattern has positive results in literacy and education, health, status of women and demographic factors. Another important aspect is that the rural–urban difference in all these social indicators, is marginal, unlike other parts of India. Let us examine these matters in detail.

Literacy

Kerala was the first Indian state to achieve total literacy. In April 1991, Kerala was formally declared 'totally literate'.[3] As is evident from the graph, Kerala had a higher literacy rate than India as a whole. The increase in literacy revealed in the 1991 census, over the 1981 census was, to a great extent, the result of the total literacy programme.[4] For a whole year, about 350,000 volunteers under the supervision of nearly 30,000 master trainers worked hard to make millions of illiterates, functionally literate (Chandran, 1994).

What makes literate Kerala more 'beautiful' (*Sakshara Keralam, Sundara Keralam* i.e., literate Kerala, beautiful Kerala was the main slogan of the campaign) is that the national literacy scene is far from beautiful! Even as in 1991, 48% of the Indian population lacks reading, writing and numerical skills.

At the national level, though the percentage of illiterates decreased from 83.33% in 1951 to 48% in 1991, the number of illiterates in absolute terms increased from 300 million to 470 million. All the more depressing is the fact that the gap between literate males and literate females has been widening since the beginning of the century. From a disparity of 9.23% in 1901, it went up to 24.84% in 1991. At the same time in Kerala, though the gap exists, it has been considerably reduced from 16% to 7.45% within the last nine decades. Of the 15 major Indian states for which literacy rates are available, 6 states (Orissa, Andhra Pradesh, Madhya Pradesh, Uttar Pradesh, Rajasthan and Bihar) were consistently below national average in male, female and persons literacy rates, since 1951 (*Economic Review,*

1993). As for the literacy of the oppressed classes, Kerala is far ahead of the national average, as is evident from Table 2.1.

Table 2.1   Percentage of literates to estimated population aged 7 years and above, 1981

	Scheduled castes		Scheduled tribes	
	Males	Females	Males	Females
Kerala	72.5	57.2	44.8	30.0
India	37.7	13.0	29.8	9.6

Source: Radhakrishnan and Akila, (1993).

Comparing Kerala with China, Sen (1993) observes that the rural literacy rates for men and women of Kerala is higher 'than in every single province in China' and that the female literacy rate of Kerala's 86% is substantially higher than China's 68%. In another comparison of India with China, Dreze and Loh (1995) brings out three major observations:

1.   India and China had very similar adult literacy rates in the late 1940s, while Kerala was far ahead at that time.
2.   By 1981–82, China had caught up with Kerala in the younger age groups, while India was left far behind,
3.   Kerala enjoys relatively high literacy rates even in older age groups, which is not the case in China (especially for women).

Demographic transition and health indicators of Kerala

Kerala is in the third stage of demographic transition, wherein both the death rates and birth rates decline resulting in a low rate of population growth. During the last hundred years, Kerala's population showed an increase of 401.72% (*Final Population Totals, Census of India*, 1991). The annual exponential growth rates for Kerala and India are 1.34 and 2.14, respectively. The decadal growth rate in 1981–91 of 14.32% in Kerala against the all India growth rate of 23.85% is the lowest among all states in India (Table 2.2).

Table 2.2   Population characteristics in Kerala and India

Period	Kerala		India	
	Decadal growth rate	Annual growth rate	Decadal growth rate	Annual growth rate
1911–21	9.16	0.90	–0.31	–0.33
1921–31	21.85	1.98	11.00	1.05
1931–41	16.04	1.50	14.23	1.14
1941–51	22.82	2.08	13.31	1.26
1951–61	24.76	2.24	21.63	1.98
1961–71	26.28	2.36	24.80	2.24
1971–81	19.24	1.78	25.00	2.26
1981–91	13.98	1.32	23.50	2.13

Source: *Economic Review*, various issues.

Fertility rates

At present, the fertility rate in Kerala is at or below replacement level (Zachariah, et. al, 1994). The fertility rate has shown considerable decline since 1971 (Table 2.3).

Table 2.3   Fertility rates – Kerala and India – 1988

	Rural	Urban	Total
Kerala	2	2.1	2
India	4.3	3.1	4

Source: *State Plan of Action for the Child in Kerala*, 1995.

Usually a combination of economic growth (growth in per capita income, economic transition (from agricultural to non-agricultural sector, rapid industrialization) social change (urbanization) and social development (high literacy, low infant and child mortality) lead to fertility decline. In Kerala, despite the fact that every aspect other than social development was absent, Kerala underwent a fertility decline. Mahadevan and Sumangala (1987) found that high age at marriage, low perceived risk of infant mortality, level of education, modernization, emancipation of women, adoption of family planning and utilization of the health care system were the factors which led to fertility decline in Kerala.

Zachariah et. al (1994) in their detailed study of the demographic profile in Kerala, observed that by 1991, Kerala woman's fertility rate depended more on age, age at marriage and the district of domicile. Other factors, like religion, level of education, financial status had become insignificant.[5]

Table 2.4   Fertility rates in Kerala (selected years)

Year	Fertility Rate
1971	4.1
1976	3.4
1981	2.8
1988	2.2
1992	1.9

Source: *State Plan of Action for the Child in Kerala*, 1995.

Table 2.5   Total fertility rates in major world regions and Kerala, 1980 and 1993

Regions	1980	1993
Developed countries	2.0	1.8
Sub-Saharan Africa	6.7	6.4
Middle-East and North Africa	5.9	4.9
South Asia	5.2	4.2
Latin America and Caribbean	4.2	3.0
East Asia Pacific	3.2	2.5
Kerala	2.8	1.9*

Key: * 1992.
Source: UNICEF, *The State of the World's Children*, Oxford and New York, Oxford University Press, 1995 and *State Plan of Action for the Child in Kerala*, 1995.

Crude birth rates

Figure 2.1   Crude birth rates for Kerala and India (selected years)

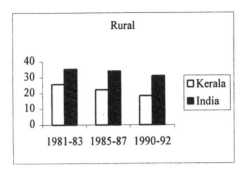

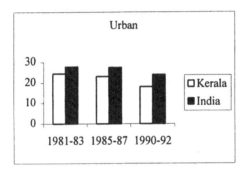

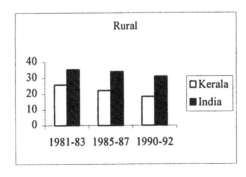

Source: Sample Registration System estimates.

During the decade of India's independence (1940–50), India's birth rate of 39.9 was not really higher than Kerala's 39.8 (*Women in Kerala*, 1978). Unlike the overall Indian scenario, the birth rate in Kerala has fallen considerably (Fig. 2.1). During a span of 25 years from 1966–91, the birth rate declined by more than half in Kerala (from 37 to 18 per 1,000 population). Kerala recorded the lowest decadal growth rate of 13.98 among all the Indian states, and Kerala has the lowest birth rate among all major Indian states.

While the birth rate has been consistently high in rural India for the period for which data is readily available, (since 1981–83), the birth rate in rural Kerala has become less than urban Kerala (Figure 2.1). In all the major states, the rural birth rate is considerably higher than the urban birth rates.

While the national target is to realize replacement level (net reproduction rate of 1) by the year AD 2000 Kerala had nearly achieved this demographic goal already by the year 1985 (Kannan et. al, 1991).

Sen's observation (1994) that Kerala's birth rate of 18 per 1,000 is actually lower than China's 19, demands more clarification. Since 1987, Kerala's birth rate has been lower than China. By 1993, China's birth rate was 18.1 against Kerala's 17.3.

Infant mortality

Any reduction in infant mortality has a direct positive bearing on life expectancy. Kerala's infant mortality rate of 17 against the all India figure of 80 during 1990–92, again is the lowest among all Indian states. There are Indian states which have infant mortality rates exceeding 100 (Orissa: 120 and Madhya Pradesh: 111). Here also the urban-rural disparity is high on a national level (rural 86 and urban 52) and at state-levels, while in Kerala, the disparity is marginal (rural: 17 and urban: 15).

Since 1981, the infant mortality rate in Kerala has almost always been less than one third of India's. In both perinatal and neonatal mortality, not only have Kerala's rates been considerably lower than the all India figures, the reduction of infant mortality at the national level has been lower than that achieved in Kerala.

Child mortality

The data for India as a whole and in Kerala for the child mortality rate per 1,000 for the period 1984–90 are given below.

Table 2.6   Child mortality rate (per 1,000)

Year	Kerala	India
1984	8.9	41.2
1985	10.2	38.4
1986	8.1	36.6
1987	7.6	35.2
1988	7.7	33.3
1989	6.1	29.9
1990	4.6	26.3

Source: *State Plan of Action for the Child in Kerala*, 1995.

WHO reported that in 1993 out of every 1,000 babies born alive, 87 died before reaching age 5 (*The World Health Report*, 1995). Considering the fact that the global average in 1995 was 81.7 (*The World Health Report*, 1996), Kerala's achievements in the reduction of child mortality are highly commendable.

Maternal mortality

According to the ninth revision of the International Classification of Diseases, a maternal death is defined as 'the death of a woman while pregnant or within 42 days of termination of pregnancy, irrespective of the duration and the site of the pregnancy, from any cause related to or aggravated by the pregnancy or its management but not from accidental or incidental causes' (Abouzhahr and Royston, 1991, cited in McNay, 1995; p. WS–83).

In developing regions, pregnancy still presents a very high risk. WHO estimates that the lifetime risk of dying from pregnancy or child-birth related causes is 1 in 20 in developing countries, compared with 1 in 10,000 in developed countries. Maternal mortality ranged from more than

600 deaths per 100,000 live births in the least developed countries to about 10 deaths per 100,000 live births in the developed countries. With 460 maternal deaths per 100,000 live births even as late as in 1990–91, maternal mortality is a significant risk Indian women are 'destined' to face (McNay, 1995). In Kerala, maternal mortality is estimated to be less than 1 per 3,000 live births (*Economic Review*, 1995), i.e., approximately 33 maternal deaths per 100,000. The chances of Indian mothers dying during the course of, or as a result of pregnancy, is roughly 14 times more than Kerala mothers. Since the institutionalization for deliveries in other parts of India is low, compared to Kerala, chances of proper recording of maternal deaths, would also be low, compared to Kerala. This leads to the possibility of maternal mortality rates in India being higher than estimated.

Figure 2.2   Maternal deaths related to child-bearing in major world regions, India and Kerala, 1990s (per 100,000)

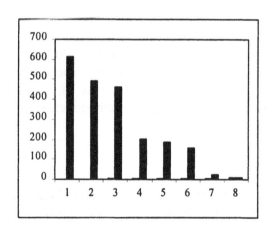

Key: 1. Sub-Saharan Africa, 2. South Asia, 3. India, 4. Middle-East and North Africa, 5. Latin America and Caribbean, 6. East Asia and Pacific, 7. Kerala, 8. Developed Countries.

Source: UNICEF, *The State of the World's Children*, Oxford and New York: Oxford University Press, 1995; *Economic and Political Weekly*, 28 October 1995; *State Plan of Action for the Child in Kerala*, 1995.

Low fertility rate, institutionalization of deliveries, use of traditional medicines, especially Ayurveda, proper pre- and post-natal maternal care, lack of gender discrimination, communication facilities – all would have contributed to the low maternal mortality in Kerala. High mean age at marriage, family planning practices (which result in low fertility rates), higher level of education and literacy, which facilitates acceptance of medical facilities are other reasons for low maternal mortality in Kerala.

Institutionalization of deliveries

In Kerala, unlike the rest of India, the majority of deliveries take place in institutions and this has contributed considerably to low infant and maternal mortality. Table 2.7 gives the percentage distribution of births by type of medical attention received by the mother at delivery. Though there still exists some disparity between rural and urban areas in institutionalization, and care by trained professionals in Kerala, the disparity is very much less than in India as a whole.

Table 2.7 Distribution of births by type of medical attention (in %)

Sector		Institutional	Attended by trained professionals	Attended by untrained professionals
Rural	Kerala	90.6	5.3	4.1
	India	17.6	20.8	61.1
Urban	Kerala	95.3	3.7	1.0
	India	53.8	26.9	19.2
Total	Kerala	91.5	5.0	3.6
	India	24.3	21.9	53.7

Death rates

The person death rate is 6.0 (*Kerala at a glance 1992*) and the urban-rural disparity is the least among all Indian states. During 1990–92, the all India rural death rate was 10.7, against 6.1 in Kerala and urban death rate 7.0 at the national level against 5.9 in Kerala.

Table 2.8   Death rates in Kerala and India (selected years)

Year	Kerala	India
1970	9.2	15.7
1980	7.0	12.6
1990	6.1	14.2
1994	6.0	9.2

Source: *Economic Review*, 1994

Extending Sen's (1994) comparison of Kerala – China death rates, it can be found that since 1986, Kerala's death rate has been lower than that of China. For example, in the year 1993, the death rate in China was 6.6 against Kerala's figure of 6.0.

Life expectancy

Expectation of life at birth of Keralites is much above the all India figures, as is evident from Figure 2.3. Furthermore, the life expectancy of Kerala is the highest among all Indian states. In Kerala, as in all developed countries, males have higher mortality than females at all ages, as is reflected in the higher life expectancy of females.

Figure 2.3   Life expectancy – Kerala and India during 1988–91

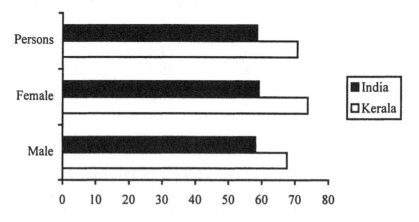

Source: Economic and Political Weekly, 21 May 1994.

After an extensive analysis of variations in survival rates by sex and region, Sen (1993) writes:

> The survival chances of the average African-American are better than those of an African-American living in Harlem, but are unfavourable when compared with those of US whites and those of the citizens of China and Kerala, who have much lower incomes. Although black woman fare better than the men do, they too fall behind women in Kerala and China as they age (p. 45).

Sex ratio

Though more males are born than females, females tend to have lower mortality. Provided of course, the social factors are conducive, there should be more females than males. In both Europe and North America, the sex ratio,[6] expressed as the number of women per 1,000 men, is favourable to women. The sex ratio in Kerala is 1,036 against the European ratio of 1,050 and Sub-Saharan African ratio of 1,020. Sen and Dreze calculated the number of women 'missing' in male deficit countries, taking the Sub-Saharan ratio as the bench mark. They found that 44 million women in China and 37 million in India are missing. The sex ratio is improving in China, though, marginally.[7]

Demographic trends indicate a comparative better status of women in Kerala. According to 1991 Census, out of the total population of 29,032,828, 14,230,391 were males and 14,802,437 were females, showing a sex ratio of 1,036 females to 1,000 males. In 1981, the sex ratio was 1,032 females to 1,000 males. The corresponding national figures for 1991 were 927 and 934 in 1981. As is evident from the Table 2.9, against the increasing masculinisation at the national level during this century, Kerala has been improving its sex ratio.

Three other major states, where there were more women than men at the beginning of the century have also joined the national masculinisation process (Table 2.10).

Another aspect of sex ratio in Kerala is that the sex ratio is favourable to women among all religions (Hindus: 1,041; Muslims: 1,048 and Christians: 1,013; *Census of India*, 1991).

Table 2.9   Sex Ratio in Kerala and India during the 20th century

	Kerala	India
1901	1004	972
1911	1008	964
1921	1011	955
1931	1022	950
1941	1027	945
1951	1028	946
1961	1022	941
1971	1016	930
1981	1032	934
1991	1036	929

Source: Saradamoni, *Kerala Padanangal*, Vol. 2, 1995.

Table 2.10   Masculinisation process in selected Indian states

	Bihar	Orissa	Tamil Nadu
1901	1054	1037	1044
1911	1044	1056	1042
1921	1016	1086	1029
1931	994	1067	1027
1941	996	1053	1012
1951	990	1022	1007
1961	994	1001	992
1971	954	988	978
1981	946	981	977
1991	912	972	972

Source: Saradamoni, K., *Kerala Padanangal*, Vol. 2, 1995.

During these last two census periods (1981 and 1991), the sex ratio for the oppressed classes – the Scheduled castes and Scheduled tribes of Kerala was also higher than the national average, showing an improvement against the declining national picture. In 1981, the sex ratio of Scheduled castes in Kerala was 1,022 (1,022 women per every 1,000 men) against the national average of 932 and in 1991, Kerala's figures were 1,029 women per 1,000 men, against the all India figure of 922 women per 1,000 men. Among the scheduled tribes of Kerala, in 1981, there were 992 women per 1,000 men and 996 women per 1,000 men in 1991, while the national figures showed a down ward trend – from 983 in 1981 to 972 in 1991. Among all Indian states, Kerala stands first in sex ratio favourable to women for scheduled caste population, scheduled tribe population, non-scheduled caste and non-scheduled tribe population and population as a whole. In a disaggregated analysis of the female/male ratio (FMR) data from the national census data across the three socio-economic groups, across different states and over four decades (1961–91), Agnihotri (1995) found that both the number and the incremental increase in the number of missing females at the national level has been showing an upward trend. The trend is the same for scheduled castes, scheduled tribes and the general population, but the incremental increase of missing females is the highest among the general population.

This means that the status of women in Kerala is much better when compared to women in India. In India, discrimination against females begins even before birth. Technological advancement (ultra-sound machines) have made identifying foetal sex and the resultant selective abortion easy. This has led to what demographer Bose describes as 'playing havoc with the sex ratio' (cited in *Asia Times*, 21 June 1996). Official Registrar General of India reports that during 1993–94, 36,000 abortions were performed on female foetuses in India. The discrimination continues against those females who survive. The systematic discrimination finds expression in neglecting and undernourishing female children, less access to medical care and when they grow up they have to undergo the risk of high reproductive rates.

In Kerala there is no female infanticide. The females born in Kerala are 'luckier' when compared to their counterparts in India. They are educated, their fertility rates and child–woman ratio are lower. They are not neglected, discriminated against or killed. Kerala proves that the biologically stronger sex can survive in developing areas, as they do in developed areas.

Other demographic indicators

Table 2.11 clearly shows that the proportion of married couples per 1,000 population in Kerala is lower than that in India, the child–woman ratio is lower and compared to India as a whole, both men and women get married later.

Table 2.11   Other demographic indicators in Kerala and India (selected years)

	1961		1971		1981	
	K	I	K	I	K	I
Married couples[a]	151	n.a.	140	170	146	165
Child–woman ratio[b]	700	659	550	655	409	546
Mean age at marriage: Male	26.3	20.0	26.7	22.4	27.7	23.4
Mean age at marriage: Female	19.8	14.5	21.1	17.2	21.9	18.7

Keys: [a] per 1,000 population; [b] per 1,000 women; K – Kerala; I – India.
Source: *Women in Kerala*, 1989.

All the demographic and health indicators described above clearly shows that Kerala is way ahead of India in all these indicators.

Provision of basic services

In comparison with the other Indian states, Kerala has an impressive record in the provision of basic services. This is evident from Table 2.12. These figures relate to the late 1970s.[8] Though the other states have improved their position during the last one and a half decades, Kerala still retains its significant position.

In a detailed study of the telecommunication scene in Kerala, Krishnaswamy (1998) established that Kerala ranks first among all Indian states in teleaccess and expressed demand.[9]

Table 2.12   Provision of basic services

Kind of service	Rank of Kerala	% of villages covered	
		Kerala	India
Within 2 kms			
All weather roads	1	98	46
Bus stops	1	98	40
Post offices	1	100	53
Primary schools	1	100	90
Secondary schools	1	99	44
Fair price shops	1	99	39
Health dispensaries	1	91	25
Health centres	1	47	12
Within 5 kms			
Higher education facilities	1	97	21
Hospitals	1	78	35
Fertilizer depots	1	93	44
Agr.pump-repair shops	1	65	19
Veterinary dispensaries	1	82	45
Co-op. credit banks	1	96	61
Other banks	1	96	40
Seed stores	2	63	40
Storage and warehouses	4	34	21
Railway stations	8	23	18
Within the village			
Drinking water	5	96	93
Electricity	3	97	33

Source: Franke and Chasin, 1990.

India and Kerala in Development Indicators

The high scores in the Human Development Index (HDI) (Table 2.13) and
Physical Quality of Life Index (PQLI) (Table 2.14) are the reasons for the
national and international attention towards development in Kerala. HDI
for three years from 1990 shows that Kerala ranks first, despite its
relatively lower rank in state domestic product (SDP).

Table 2.13   Human Development Index for Indian states

States	HDI 1990	HDI 1991	HDI 1992	Per Capita SDP
Andhra Pradesh	0.361	0.3397	0.3928	5,570
Assam	0.256	0.2452	0.4441	4,230
Bihar	0.147	0.1334	0.2118	2,904
Gujarat	0.566	0.5453	0.4950	6,424
Haryana	0.624	0.5995	0.6626	8,690
Himachal Pradesh	0.425	0.4805	–	5,355
Jammu and Kashmir	0.109	0.1601	–	4,051
Karnataka	0.502	0.4772	0.4658	5,555
Kerala	**0.775**	**0.7749**	**0.7343**	**4,618**
Madhya Pradesh	0.196	0.1863	0.0858	4,077
Maharashtra	0.655	0.6430	0.6116	8,180
Orissa	0.224	0.2132	0.2960	4,068
Punjab	0.744	0.7131	0.7215	9,463
Rajasthan	0.246	0.2294	0.3231	4,361
Tamil Nadu	0.508	0.4873	0.4985	5,078
Uttar Pradesh	0.110	0.1095	0.2892	4,012
West Bengal	0.436	0.4176	0.5318	5,383

Note: * at current prices in Indian currency.
Source: Adapted from *Economic and Political Weekly*, 21 May 1994.

Table 2.14   Rural and Urban PQLIs for the major Indian states (1971 and 1991)

	PQLI (1971)			PQLI (1991)		
	Urban	Rural	Total	Urban	Rural	Total
Andhra Pradesh	62	39	43	29.41	44.20	42.70
Assam with Meghalaya	64	35	37	44.03	68.70	29.60
Bihar	–	–	–	22.77	22.54	18.17
Gujarat	55	34	40	50.47	57.96	58.38
Haryana	–	–	–	54.26	54.52	55.68
Karnataka	65	43	48	39.80	39.70	39.55
Kerala	**74**	**69**	**70**	**77.79**	**91.52**	**89.11**
Madhya Pradesh	60	32	37	24.09	15.79	16.08
Maharashtra	62	42	49	59.95	46.68	53.27
Orissa	59	35	37	28.12	8.60	6.70
Punjab	65	48	50	61.54	65.10	66.28
Rajasthan	58	28	33	25.68	29.64	28.41
Tamil Nadu	64	39	46	51.62	44.48	48.09
Uttar Pradesh	49	21	25	9.32	17.90	15.39
West Bengal	–	–	–	55.55	45.97	48.31
All-India average	61	35	40	41.52	34.84	36.14

Source: Adapted from *Economic and Political Weekly*, 21 May 1994.

National Performance Gaps

In 1995, the United Nations measured the national performance gaps of 130 countries by comparing the Human Development Index (comprising of life expectancy, adult literacy and GNP per capita) with GNP per capita income. The study found that 60 countries 'did not (fully) translate their wealth into social benefits'. Of the 70 countries which have been successful in translating wealth into benefits for their citizens, Sri Lanka ranks first, with a positive score of 50, followed by China, scoring 44 and Vietnam, with 40. On the negative side Oman ranked first with 56 points, followed by United Arab Emirates 50 and Gabon 46.

Table 2.15   National Performance Gap of the richest 10 countries

Country	GNP rank	HDI rank	Disparity gap
Switzerland	1	3	−2
USA	2	19	−17
Norway	3	6	−3
U.A.E.	4	56	−50
Japan	5	1	4
Sweden	6	2	4
Canada	7	5	2
Denmark	8	9	−1
Kuwait	9	43	−34
Finland	10	11	−1

Source: 'National Performance Gaps', *The Progress of Nations*, 1996, World Wide Web.

Again, of the richest 10 countries, only 3 countries, Japan, Sweden and Canada have positive scores and of the remaining 7 countries, the disparity gap is highest in United Arab Emirates (−50), followed by Kuwait (−34). Surprisingly the third place in negative disparity goes to the United States of America (−17) (Table 2.15).

Here the comparisons are not strictly between economic development and social development, because one-third of the Human Development Index is the economic factor of per capita GNP, which does not in fact reveal the possible skewed distribution of income.

Economic development – social development disparity

To put Kerala development in perspective, to analyze whether Kerala's development experience is different from other regions of the country and to find out whether Kerala has achieved social development higher than that which could be expected from its economic growth, an economic development–social development disparity measure is introduced. The following analysis shows how far each Indian state has been successful in transforming its economic growth into social development. The positive and negative disparity levels are arrived at, after finding out the expected level of social development in relation to the per capita state domestic product of the major Indian states.

There are two fundamental questions relevant here. Can social development take place at low levels of income? Can high economic development ensure high social development? It is obvious from Table 2.16 that economic growth alone need not result in social development. There are both positive and negative disparities among the states.

Table 2.16   Economic and social development indicators of the major Indian states

States	Per capita SDP	PQLI
Andhra Pradesh	4,728	42.70
Assam	4,014	44.03
Bihar	2,655	18.17
Gujarat	5,687	58.38
Haryana	7,502	55.68
Karnataka	4,696	39.55
Kerala	**4,207**	**89.11**
Madhya Pradesh	4,149	16.08
Maharashtra	7,316	53.27
Orissa	3,077	6.70
Punjab	8,373	66.28
Rajasthan	4,113	28.41
Tamil Nadu	5,047	48.09
Uttar Pradesh	3,516	15.39
West Bengal	4,753	48.31

Keys: Per capita state domestic product (SDP) figures are for 1990–91; Physical Quality of Life Index (PQLI) are for 1991.
Source: Centre for Monitoring Indian Economy, *Basic Statistics: States*, 1994; *Economic and Political Weekly*, 21 May 1994.

Statistical analysis

Per capita State Domestic Product (SDP) is used as the economic development indicator and PQLI as the social development indicator. A linear function is chosen relating social development (Y) to per capita SDP (X).

$$Y = a + bX$$

where 'a' is the intercept and 'b' the slope and is estimated with ordinary least squares. Parameter estimates for equation (1) are given in equation (2) with 't' values indicated in parenthesis.

$$R^2 = 0.369444$$
$$Y = 1.884474 + 0.008152X$$
$$(0.123308) \ (2.759842)$$

Kerala, whose social development exceeds the *expected* (i.e., PQLI is greater than that predicted by SDP), has a positive value of economic development–social development disparity. Kerala has been successful in converting economic resources into social development. The value of economic development–social development disparity for Kerala is highly significant at 3 standard deviations. On the other hand, Orissa has been unsuccessful in translating its economic development into social development. Orissa's economic development–social development disparity is negatively significant at 1 standard deviation (Table 2.17).

Thus the crux of Kerala's development experience is that Kerala *has achieved high physical quality of life* in terms of literacy, life expectancy and infant mortality, *at low per capita income*.

The definition of the Kerala model is not clear. When the Kerala model is defined as high social development and low economic growth, it implies that there is a causal relationship between high social development and low economic development. If on the other hand, the definition centres around high social development at low economic growth, the model has positive connotations. If economic growth is a necessary condition (though not a sufficient condition) for social development, it would be appropriate to define the Kerala model as high social development despite low economic growth.

The Indian experience shows that there is no state that has attained high economic development and high social development. Rather, Kerala's high PQLI and HDI scores in the Indian context show that though Kerala's policies have not succeeded in increasing economic development, Kerala has succeeded in improving the quality of living of its people. It shows that countries need not wait for economic development in order to intervene in social sectors. Several Indian states, which have followed different development strategies, have neither succeeded in attaining economic development nor social development. Those states, which have succeeded in increasing growth (for example, Punjab and Haryana), have not succeeded in the social sectors. While it is true that both economic and social aspects of development should go hand in hand, the Indian reality is far from the ideal state.

Table 2.17 Values of economic development – social development disparity

States	Actual PQLI	Predicted PQLI	Residuals	Remarks
Andhra Pradesh	42.70	40.42689	2.273109	
Assam	44.03	34.6064	9.423601	
Bihar	18.17	23.5279	−5.3579	
Gujarat	58.38	48.24461	10.13539	
Haryana	55.68	63.0404	−7.3604	
Karnataka	39.55	40.16603	−0.61603	
Kerala	**89.11**	**36.17973**	**52.93027**	**significant at 3 std. deviation**
Madhya Pradesh	16.08	35.70691	−19.6269	
Maharashtra	53.27	61.52414	−8.25414	
Orissa	6.70	26.96802	−20.268	significant at 1 std. deviation
Punjab	66.28	70.14075	−3.86075	
Rajasthan	28.41	35.41344	−7.00344	
Tamil Nadu	48.09	43.02736	5.062637	
Uttar Pradesh	15.39	30.54673	−15.1567	
West Bengal	48.31	40.63069	7.67931	

Scholars have attributed several different reasons for the high social development of Kerala. They are: public policy and female education (Sen, 1994), public interventionist policies on poverty and social development (Centre for Development Studies [CDS], 1975); citizens' participation in policy making and implementation (Alvis, 1991); the class struggle led by the communist party against local reactionary forces (Amin, 1991); communist led radical mass organization (Patnaik, 1991); favourable geographic factors, indigenous tradition of knowledge and diffusion of knowledge, British colonialism and people's struggles for rights (Ram Mohan, 1991), protest movements (Parvathamma, 1986); land reforms (Alexander, 1974); women and government intervention (Caldwell, 1986); social welfare programmes (Nayar, 1983); women and literacy (*Economic and Political Weekly*, 21 May 1994); and the foundations for social development laid by the erstwhile princely rulers (Zachariah and Suryamoorthy, 1994). It was a combination of historical, cultural and geographical factors, coupled with the aspirations of the people and social welfare, redistribution and public policies of state governments (most communist governments and coalition governments in which the communists had significant role) which contributed to the high social development in Kerala.

The Paradox of Kerala model of development

Economy

> ... let not the praise that scholars shower on Kerala for its achievements divert attention from the intense economic crisis that we face. We are behind other states of India in respect of economic growth, and a solution to this crisis brooks no delay (p. 5).

The above words of Namboodiripad (1994) reflect the dilemma of Kerala development experience. Unlike Brazil in the seventies, in Kerala 'people are supposed to be doing fine, but the economy is not'.[10] It is this paradox that has led economists to question sustainability (Kannan, 1990; and George, K.K., 1994); highlight the limitations (Adiseshiah,[11] 1978 and Eapen, 1994) and doubt the prioritization (Gulati, 1995) of the Kerala model of development.

Let us examine the state of the Kerala economy. The state income has been growing at a slower rate compared to the growth in national income. As Gulati (1995) rightly points out Kerala's economic growth has been only about half of national level growth. While the national income in real terms grew by 68% between 1981 and 1991, Kerala's improvement was only 38% (Gulati, 1995).

The per capita income of Kerala and India as a whole for the period 1980–81 to 1994–95 are given below.

The state income has been growing at a slower rate compared to the growth of national income. The share of state domestic product in addition to the national domestic product shrunk from 3.46% in 1980–81 to 3.02% in 1992–93 (Table 2.18).

Table 2.18 **Net Domestic Product at 1980–81 prices – India and Kerala**

Year	India	Kerala	share (%)
1980–81	1,103.40	38.23	3.46
81–82	1,171.01	37.35	3.18
82–83	1,203.20	38.26	3.17
83–84	1,303.96	36.71	2.81
84–85	1,349.85	38.98	2.88
85–86	1,402.26	40.86	2.91
86–87	1,459.78	39.38	2.67
87–88	1,519.88	41.66	2.74
88–89	1,689.85	45.84	2.71
89–90	1,806.86	48.92	2.70
90–91	1,902.41	52.69	2.76
91–92	1,907.80	56.08	2.93
92–93	1,988.33	60.23	3.02

Key: Rupees in billions.
Source: *Economic and Political Weekly*, 23 December 1995.

From 1980–81 to 1993–94, Kerala's per capita income was lower than the national per capita income. While the national per capita income grew by 80.20% from 1981–82 to 1993–94, Kerala's growth in per capita income during the same period was only 61.26%. When we take into account the demographic transition of Kerala, where the growth rate of population has been considerably less than the all India growth rate (Kerala: 1.8% and India, almost 2.4%), Kerala has been really lagging behind the all India average (Table 2.19). In other words, if Kerala had the same population growth of the country, the per capita income would have been considerably less and the growth in per capita income would have been insignificant, if not nil.

In 1980–81 prices, while Kerala was lagging behind India by Rs. 136 in 1980–81, by 1993–94, Kerala was lagging behind the national average by Rs. 314. Punjab, Haryana, Gujarat and Maharashtra have higher per capita incomes when compared to the all India per capita figure. The other three major south Indian states of Karnataka, Tamil Nadu and Andhra Pradesh have begun to touch the national average (Table 2.20).

Table 2.19   Per capita net Domestic Product at 1980–81 prices – India and Kerala

Year	India	Kerala	Difference
1980–81	1,630	1,494	136
1981–82	1,693	1,453	240
1982–83	1,691	1,462	229
1983–84	1,790	1,377	413
1984–85	1,811	1,435	376
1985–86	1,841	1,462	379
1986–87	1,871	1,400	471
1987–88	1,901	1,413	488
1988–89	2,059	1,501	558
1989–90	2,157	1,560	697
1990–91	2,223	1,802	421
1991–92	2,178	1,891	287
1992–93	2,226	1,932	294
1993–94	2,282	1,968	314

Source: *Economic and Political Weekly*, 23 December 1995.

Table 2.20 highlights the difference in growth per capita net state domestic product between major Indian states for the decade ending 1990. Kerala, which had the 8th rank in 1980–91, had 9th rank by 1990–91. As for the growth percentage rank, only West Bengal is ranked below Kerala. Growth over the decade was only 20.61%.

The government of Kerala consoles itself that though 'the per capita income of the state continues to lag behind the national average, (but) during the last few years the gap between the two has been steadily declining' (*Economic Review*, 1993, 1995).

Table 2.20   Per capita net state Domestic Product at 1980–81 prices and relative ranking – major Indian states

States	1980–81	Rank	1990–91	Rank
Andhra Pradesh	1,380	9	1,752	11
Assam	1,200	14	1,774	10
Bihar	878	15	1,177	15
Gujarat	1,951	4	2,525	4
Haryana	2,370	3	3,405	2
Karnataka	1,596	6	2,024	6
Kerala	**1,494**	**8**	**1,802**	**9**
Madhya Pradesh	1,325	10	1,696	12
Maharashtra	2,427	2	3,281	3
Orissa	1,231	12	1,557	14
Punjab	2,675	1	3,676	1
Rajasthan	1,222	13	1,890	8
Tamil Nadu	1,498	7	2,025	5
Uttar Pradesh	1,286	11	1,588	13
West Bengal	1,612	5	1,917	7
All India	1,630		3,420	

Source: *Economic and Political Weekly*, 23 December 1995.

Table 2.21 Per capita net Domestic Product of major Indian states at 1980–81 – growth percentage and relative ranking

States	Growth %	Rank
Andhra Pradesh	26.95	10
Assam	47.83	2
Bihar	34.05	7
Gujarat	29.42	8
Haryana	43.67	3
Karnataka	26.81	11
Kerala	**20.61**	**14**
Madhya Pradesh	28.00	9
Maharashtra	35.18	5
Orissa	26.48	12
Punjab	37.42	4
Rajasthan	54.66	1
Tamil Nadu	35.18	6
Uttar Pradesh	23.48	13
West Bengal	18.92	15

Source: *Economic and Political Weekly*, 23 December 1995.

Sectoral analysis of Kerala economy

The primary sector (consisting of agriculture, livestock, fisheries, forestry and mining and quarrying) is declining, the secondary sector (i.e., manufacturing, construction, and electricity generation and water supply) is stagnant and only the tertiary sector (essentially service sector, which includes transport, storage and communication, trade, business and other services) is improving its share in state domestic product (Table 2.22). Though the remittances from Keralites both abroad and in other states, are not reflected in state domestic product, it is reflected in the tertiary sector. This essentially means that the growth in the tertiary sector is not from the primary and secondary sectors of the state. This lop-sided economic development has contributed to fiscal crisis and unemployment in Kerala.

**Table 2.22   Sectoral classification of net Domestic Product of Kerala
– selected years (in %)**

Sector	1980–81	1990–91	1994–95
Primary	39.23	35.99	32.33
Secondary	24.37	23.92	25.22
Tertiary	36.40	40.09	42.45

Source: Computed from *Economic Review*, 1995.

Fiscal crisis in Kerala

During the 1980s, in Kerala, the Government treasury had to be literally closed down a couple of times due to fiscal crisis. This was because the Reserve Bank of India suspended state government's treasury payments, where there had been a delay in the repayment of over-draft instalments on loans made to state governments. As a result, the government of Kerala controls expenditure tightly, to avoid fiscal breakdown.

Kerala is in an acute debt trap. Debt servicing payments take away 87% of the new central government loans. The per capita debt[12] outstanding is not only higher than the all states average, but is also increasing (Table 2.23).

Table 2.23   Per capita debt outstanding – Kerala and all states

	1988	1989	1990	1991	1992	1993	1994
Kerala	994	1010	1191	1491	1775	2052	2371
All states	884	1004	1126	1303	1479	1640	1817

Source: *Kerala Budget in Brief*, 1995–96.

In the federal system of India, central government fund transfers have a vital role in the state's development process. To put the entire blame for Kerala's economic stagnation on the central government may not be fair, but the central government has neglected Kerala to a great extent.

In an excellent analysis of central transfers to Kerala for the period 1974–75 to 1989–90, George, K.K. (1993) established that:

1. Except during the year 1974–75, the proportion of aggregate expenditure and revenue expenditure financed by the central government was lower than for All States (i.e., national average).
2. Kerala has also been receiving less tax share than 'all states'. Carrying forward George's analysis, we find that in 1990–91 and 1991–92 , Kerala got a 20% share while the national average was 21%. In 1992–93 against the all state average of 22% Kerala still got 20% and in 1993–94, Kerala's share was reduced to 18%, the national average remaining 22%.
3. The central government has failed to take into account the development pattern followed by Kerala where social sectors were given priority, the result of which has created 'second generation problems' like a high level of unemployment among the educated and social aspects of a greying society like taking care of the elderly and widows.

Further, the state-wise per capita assistance disbursed by all India financial institutions are also less than the national average. For example, in 1992–93, the assistance to Kerala was Rs. 56.30 against the national average of 197.70 and in 1993–94, it was 73.70 against the national average of Rs. 232.50. Despite the fact that there had been a 355% increase on deposits in nationalized and state bank groups during the period 1988–95, the credit deposit ratio decreased from 62.76% in 1988 to 44.24% in 1995. Of the total deposits in 1995, 44.60% were from non-resident Indians, which means that they are hard-earned foreign currency. Based on this low CD ratio we can assume that not only economic growth suffers, but money from the state goes out of the state (calculated from *Economic Review*, 1995).

Unemployment

Kerala ranks first among all Indian states in the indices of unemployment, suicides and female crimes and ranks high in poverty, reflecting the paradox of the Kerala model of development.

Satya (1993) in a study of the temporal and regional variations of unemployment found that Kerala has the highest level of unemployment and underemployment among all Indian states in intensity and distribution by any measure. The figures for 1983 reveal that the Person Rate of Unemployment (PRU) was 50.40 per cent and Time Rate of Unemployment (TRU) was 19.68 per cent against the all India average of 21.59 per cent and 7.51 per cent respectively.[13]

George, K.K. (1994) writes that the rate of unemployment for the period 1977–78 was between 17.07 to 21.19 per cent (depending on how it was recorded) as against 3.77 to 6.09 for all India.

Nearly four million people (3,964,000) had registered[14] themselves as job seekers in the Government's Employment Exchanges, as on 30.9.1992 (Government of Kerala, 1993). This will not give the exact picture, for, several of the people registered may not be unemployed, and several unemployed might not have registered or renewed their registration in time. The unemployment scenario in Kerala is qualitatively different considering the educational level of the job seekers. More than 100,000 professional and technical job seekers including medical and engineering graduates, diploma holders in engineering, agricultural and veterinary graduates had registered for employment in 1991 (Prakash, 1994).

Compared to the rate of registration in employment exchanges in Kerala, the rate of placement through the exchanges is too low. For the period 1985–94, while the number of candidates increased by 62%, placements through Employment Exchanges increased only by 34%. Table 2.24 shows the number registered and number of placements through employment exchanges.

Table 2.24   Candidates registered and placed through employment exchanges (in numbers)

Year	Candidates registered	Placements
1985	2,574,074	13,700
1986	2,704,874	15,571
1987	2,991,002	13,869
1988	2,901,051	15,504
1989	3,092,031	17,514
1990	3,320,035	14,280
1991	3,638,804	15,640
1992	3,847,063	17,890
1993	4,156,892	13,828
1994	4,168,669	18,305

Source: *Economic Review*, 1995.

Over the years, the increase in employment in the public sector and private sector has only been marginal. When we take into account the demand for jobs and the employment in the public and private sector in Kerala, we get a dismal picture.

**Table 2.25 Employment in the public and private sectors
(in numbers)**

Year	Public sector	Private sector	Total
1985	568,713	507,375	1,076,088
1986	576,784	519,115	1,095,899
1987	585,391	508,917	1,094,308
1988	602,696	501,653	1,104,349
1989	620,254	486,354	1,106,608
1990	634,379	512,034	1,146,413
1991	645,856	525,882	1,171,738
1992	647,853	523,837	1,180,690
1993	649,199	536,480	1,185,679

Source: Directorate of Employment and Training, *Economic Review*, 1995.

Table 2.25 reveals that the number of people employed in the public and private sectors put together is lower than the number of people waiting for jobs. In 1987, the Department of Economics and Statistics conducted a survey to assess the employment situation in Kerala. It was found that the number of chronically unemployed persons was 2.78 millions (against 2.99 millions registered in the exchanges during the year) with 1.53 million underemployed. Including the number of underemployed, the total number of unemployed comes to over 4.3 million, against the labour force of 10.75 million. Nearly 3 persons depend on one employed person.

The unemployment situation among professional and technical personnel in Kerala is also bleak. In 1994 alone, 3,494 medical graduates, 10,420 engineering graduates, 30,720 engineering and technical diploma holders, 80,757 ITI certificate holders, 4,001 agricultural graduates and 214 veterinary graduates were registered in the professional employment exchange. The increase in the rate of registration of professional work seekers over a decade from 1985 is given below.

Table 2.26 Labour activity status in Kerala (during 1987)

Activity status	Rural	Urban	Total
Employed	56.25	8.19	64.44
Underemployed	13.47	1.81	15.28
Unemployed	22.84	4.97	27.81
Total labour force	92.56	14.97	107.53
Not in labour force	148.83	21.22	170.05
Total population	241.39	36.19	277.58

Table 2.27 Increase in the rate of registration of professional graduates in Kerala (in %)

Medical graduates	305%
Engineering graduates	357%
Diploma Holders in Engineering and Technical	273%
ITI certificate holders	152%
Agricultural graduates	2,838%
Veterinary graduates	856%
Total	193%

The female labour participation rates in Kerala have also gone down compared to the national figures (Kumar, R., 1994). While Kerala women's work force participation rate had been slightly higher than the national average in 1971 (14.6 per cent against the all India figure of 14.2 per cent), in 1981 it was 16.6 per cent against the national average of 19.8 per cent and in 1991 it again went down to 16.9 per cent against the national figure of 22.7 per cent. The Government of Kerala's figure of 15.85 per cent for the period 1985–91 is considerably lower than the all India figure of 22.25 per cent (Government of Kerala, 1993). Kumar, R. (1994) observes that the increase in the female population depressed work force participation rates and increased the number of potential job seekers. Industrialization resulted in the waning of demand for female labour and systematic displacement of women from their traditional avenues of employment in agriculture and household industry. In the absence of growth in the service sector, new forms of employment for women are not generated. Kumar, R. thus sheds light into another paradox of Kerala model of development:

On the one hand, a wide range of socio-economic changes have encouraged women to offer their labour on the market. On the other, the structural changes brought about by the growth process have imposed severe limits on the prospects of women continuing to participate in the labour force at a high level. This duality is, in the end, just another feature of Kerala's distinctive pattern of development (p. 3253).

Paradox of labour scarcity in selective sectors despite severe macro unemployment

There is a preference for employment in the organized sector among Keralites. On the one hand, this can be attributed to 'white collar job' aspirations and on the other, to the security and promotion chances associated with government and public sector jobs. Education has withdrawn people from doing manual labour with the result that temporary migrant casual workers from Tamil Nadu are engaged in manual labour in several sectors like construction in Kerala.

Poverty

Unemployment has its impact on the level and intensity of poverty. According to Economic and Political Weekly Research Foundation (1994), during the period 1971–91, 28 per cent of the population in Kerala were below the poverty line against 14.3 per cent in Punjab, the state second in PQLI. Differences in definitions and methodologies used have resulted in wide variations in the estimates of poverty. A study conducted by Dandekar and Rath (1971, cited in Shaw, 1983) found that 80 per cent of the population were poor and Kerala had the widest extent of poverty. Other studies give a better, though not a good picture. The study by the CDS (CDS, 1977, cited in Prakash, 1994) using the poverty norm of 2,200 calories per capita per day, estimated that 50.5 per cent of the population were undernourished in 1961–62. An official study by the State Planning Board (*SPB*, 1978, cited in Prakash, 1994), using 2,400 calories per capita per day measurement found 63.4 per cent of the population to be undernourished. Another official study for 1977–78 (*SPB*, 1980, cited in Prakash, 1994), using 2,400 calories per capita per person for urban areas and 2,100 calories for rural areas estimated 73 per cent to be undernourished.

Repeated surveys conducted by the National Nutrition Monitoring Bureau during 1980–90 (Economic Review, 1993) revealed that in Kerala, the intake of cereals and millets was below the recommended level by 20%, pulses by 55%, green leafy vegetables, about 77.5%, milk about 42% and Vitamin A, 60%. These surveys also revealed that 47.4% of children suffered from a mild form of malnutrition, 32.9% from moderate form of malnutrition and 2% from severe form of malnutrition. The percentage of normal children was only 17.7%. Though there has been an improvement in nutrition status from 1975–79, as Table 2.28 shows, the nutrition situation among children is not satisfactory.

Despite the differences in estimates, it can be safely interpreted that the incidence of poverty and resultant undernourishment is high in Kerala.

Table 2.28   Distribution of children, aged 1–5, in Kerala according to Nutritional Grades* (in %)

Classification	Period	Normal	Mild	Moderate	Severe
Boys	1975–79	7.5	32.4	49.9	10.2
	1988–90	16.6	47.7	33.3	2.4
Girls	1975–79	7.4	39.0	43.0	10.4
	1988–90	18.8	47.1	32.5	1.6
Children	1975–79	7.5	35.7	46.5	10.3
	1988–90	17.7	47.4	32.9	2.0

Key: *NCHS Children-standard.
Source: National Nutrition Monitory Bureau Report of Repeat Surveys 1988–90, cited in *Economic Review*, 1993; p. 149.

Other social issues

George, K.K. (1994) citing a study conducted by Vadakkamcheri (1994) states that suicide rates in Kerala are three and a half times that of India. Saradamoni (1994) ascribes unemployment, mental ailments and 'Gulf syndrome' (separation of families due to emigration to Gulf countries) as the main reason for the high incidence of suicides in Kerala. During the period 1989–93, 1,517 people in Kerala committed suicide due to 'bankruptcy or sudden change in economic status' and unemployment led 970 to commit suicide[15] (*Women in Kerala*, 1994).

Kerala's achievements in social development have contributed to some 'success induced second generation problems' (George, K.K., 1994), unique to Kerala. Kerala has reached a stage of 'high morbidity, low mortality'[16] (Panickar and Soman, 1984). The disease profile in Kerala, the researchers found, has changed with the emergence of new categories of degenerative and neoplastic diseases, such as hypertension, cardio-vascular disease and cancer. A detailed Kerala Sastra Sahithya Parishad (KSSP) survey in 1987 (Kannan et. al, 1991) also endorsed this finding.

Among the Indian states, Kerala has the highest proportion of the aged as of 1990 (8.10 per cent of the population) and it is projected that this percentage will rise to more than 15 by 2020, still maintaining the lead. Kerala has 70 old age homes, out of the 329 old age homes in India as of 1989, constituting 21 per cent. (James, 1994). Thus not only that Kerala is referred to as the 'grey state of India', development writers ask whether the elderly are 'assets or liabilities' (James, 1994) and whether Kerala 'can afford to grow old' (George, K.K., 1993).

The sex ratio in Kerala is favourable to women (1,036 women for every 1,000 men; 1,146 women to 1,000 men for the 60+ category) and the large age gap between marriage partners has resulted in a high incidence of widows. With Kerala's large immigrant population, widows are left to fend for themselves and the meagre widow's pension (Rs. 65–85) reaches only 24.4 per cent of the 500,000 widows below the poverty line (Radhakrishnan, 1994).[17]

Education

The quality of school education in Kerala leaves much to be desired. A survey by KSSP in Trivandrum District to assess the level of degeneration came up with some shocking revelations. A simple test on language and numeracy was conducted among 134,784 students from 3rd standard to 7th standard in 529 schools and the results showed that more than one third of the students (35.27%) scored less than 12 marks out of a 100. The extent of illiteracy among primary and secondary schools in Kerala, is shocking. Another study in Kasargodu found that nearly 60% of the third and fourth standards (primary) were illiterates. Another study of grade four students (primary) revealed that only 18.48 per cent of students scored 50 marks and above (out of 100) in mathematics and 42.44 per cent of students achieved similar results in Malayalam (Varghese, 1994, cited in Acharya, 1995).

High morbidity and low mortality

Kannan et. al (1991) from a study on health and development in rural Kerala, found an inverse relationship between the rate of morbidity and socio-economic status. The rate of morbidity for the 'poor' was 40 per cent higher than the rate for the 'better off'. They also found that higher rate of morbidity in rural Kerala was more due to diseases of poverty than degenerative diseases – a manifestation of Kerala's continued economic backwardness and poverty of the masses. As they suggest, interventions in the health sector may have to focus on the preventive aspects of health care especially in the area of safe drinking water and provision of sanitary facilities.

The government admits that diarrhoea related problems constitute a major cause of morbidity among children *(State Plan of Action for the Child in Kerala*, 1995). In the study conducted by the DHS, it was found that diarrhoea cases constitute 23% of the total morbidity among children under age five (p. 11). Acute respiratory infection has been found to be the number one cause of morbidity in Kerala. Government has evolved new strategies for tackling the problem. These strategies include provision of smokeless stoves (*chulas*) to reduce smoke pollution inside the house and pollution control in factories and from motor vehicles.

Conclusion

Our discussion so far reveals the complexities and paradoxes of social development in Kerala. Development writers like Sen, Franke and Hellar, to name a few, have praised Kerala's achievements in social sectors. At the same time, political leaders of Kerala, like Namboodiripad and Antony have questioned the very basis of the 'Kerala model' of development. Namboodiripad, whose party (CPI-M) was, to a great extent instrumental in implementing land reforms and introducing several social welfare measures, criticizes the development path as a path of deindustrialization.

The literacy figures show that Kerala had a head start at the beginning of the century. Kerala's achievements in literacy have attracted the attention of development economists like Sen and Dreze. But their observations are based on government statistics. The quality aspects of the literacy of school children have not been considered in praising Kerala's literacy achievements. One reason for the low performance of Kerala's school going children could be the promotion policy which limits the failures in each class to 10 per cent or less of the number of students attending the class. On the positive side, this has helped in retaining children in school, with the result that the drop-out rates in Kerala are negligible. On the negative side, the performance of school-going children, leaves much to be desired. While Kerala's scores in literacy are quantitatively excellent, and are well documented in development literature, there is a conspicuous absence of any discussion on the qualitative aspects.

The fertility rate in Kerala is at or below the replacement level, very unusual for a region with low economic development. In comparison with the national figures, Kerala's birth rates, infant, child and mortality rates have been considerably reduced, due to the accessibility and utlization of the health care system. The death rate in Kerala is lower, and the life expectancy for both men and women, is higher than the national average. The national census data shows that during all the nine decades, Kerala's sex ratio was favourable to women,[18] unlike the rest of India. At the same time, the sex ratio among scheduled tribes of Kerala is in favour of men.

Both in PQLI and HDI, Kerala scores higher than other major Indian states. The statistical analysis of economic development–social development disparity shows that Kerala has achieved higher social development (expressed in PQLI), than would be expected based on its SDP. But the economic condition of Kerala is far from satisfactory. In comparison with the national income, the state income has been growing at a slower rate. The government of Kerala underwent several fiscal crises during the last decade and is still in an acute debt-trap.

The slow economic growth has resulted in severe unemployment, even among professionally qualified engineers and doctors. The female labour participation rate is lower than the national average. Institutionalization of the aged is also on the increase, as is reflected in the increasing number of old-age homes in Kerala. Again, the high morbidity rates, despite low mortality considerably change the picture of an overall healthy society.

Thus the paradox of development in Kerala is at least two-dimensional. Kerala has achieved high PQLI and HDI scores at low economic growth. However, the achievements in human development have not been translated into economic growth, which is highly essential to the very sustainability of human development.

This chapter has highlighted some of the achievements and failures of the Kerala development pattern. Most of the literature on Kerala development attributes the achievements to the pragmatic role of state governments, especially the communist governments. In the next chapter, we shall discuss the role and contribution of the state government towards the high development scores.

Notes

1   *Poverty, Unemployment and Development Policy, A Case study of selected issues with reference to Kerala*, 1975.
2   Quoted verbatim.
3   As per the National Literacy Mission's norms, any Indian state achieving 90% literacy among the age group of 15–35 is a 'totally literate' state. Kerala went beyond the National Literacy Mission norms by achieving 90% literacy among the age group of 15–60 rather than just the 15–35 year old (Krishnakumar, 1994).
4   During the first phase of the literacy mission, 1.6 million illiterate Keralites became neo-literates (Radhakrishnan, 1996).
5   Their study found that some districts have a lower fertility rate than others in Kerala; for example, the difference between Ernakulam and Malappuram, is about one and half children per woman.
6   Throughout this thesis, the term 'sex ratio' is used to denote the number of women per 1,000 men. This definition is in conformity with the Indian Censuses, which, following the British Censuses, define 'sex ratio' as the number of females to males.
7   In China, the sex ratio was 925 women per 1,000 men in 1949, and 958 women per 1,000 men in 1993. Since 1989 there have been more women than in the past: 939 women per 1,000 men in 1989; 941 in 1990; 947 in 1991; 955 in 1992 and 958 in 1993; (computed from Table on 'Population by Sex' – Wong and MacPherson, 1995).
8   More recent figures are not available.
9   Existing number of telephones plus demand as reflected in the waiting list.
10 Reference to the comments of Brazilian President on Brazilian economy - the economy is doing fine, but the people are not.
11 As early as in 1978, Dr. Malcom Adiseshiah had written: 'The Kerala model has reached its operational limits. On its solid achievements it now needs to be

supplemented and strengthened by improvement and increased use of Kerala's resources' (cited in Vijayanand, 1995; p. 48).

12   Internal debt plus loans and advances from central government plus provident fund - this excludes the per capita debt of a Keralite on Indian government's borrowings from various sources.

13   PRU and TRU are the two measures traditionally used for measuring unemployment. PRU is formally defined as PRU= n/N, where 'n' is the total number of unemployed and 'N' is the total number of persons in the labour force. This measure ignores the intensity of unemployment suffered by each unemployed person.

$$TRU = [\sum_{i=1}^{n}(m0i - m1i)] / m00$$

$where\ m0i = m1i + m2i; m1i$

being the number of days a week a person is in gainful employment and $m2i$
being the number of days a week when the person was not working, but was available

for work at current rates of wages. $m00 = \sum_{i=1}^{N} m0i$

TRU ignores the distribution of unemployed according to their intensities.

14   It is possible that the rate of registration is higher in Kerala than in the other Indian states.

15   Computed from Table 5.3 (pp. 68–69) of *Women in Kerala, 1994*. Original source: Police Department.

16   *EPW* Research Foundation (1994) observes that high morbidity in Kerala 'is probably reflective of what Gopalan (1985) hypothesised: "Economic development and removal of poverty are basic requisites for better nutrition; 'social development' and even female literacy can be no proxy for this"' (p. 1301).

17   The widow's pension was revised to Rs. 100 in 1995.

18   At the same time Kerala's sex ratio of 1,036 women per 1,000 men is lower than the European rate of 1,050 women per 1,000 men.

3 The Government and Social Sector in Kerala

In the last chapter we established that Kerala has achieved a PQLI higher than would be expected of its SDP. In this chapter, the role of state government in social sectors will be analyzed. The statistical analysis as to whether the Kerala government's expenditure on social sectors is more than that is expected of its gross state domestic product will help to evaluate the role of state government. Before analyzing the statistical significance, we will discuss the contribution of state government in providing education, health care and social security.

Provision of education

In 1817, Rani Laxmi Bayi of Travancore proclaimed that 'the state shall defray the entire cost of education of its people in order that there may be no backwardness in the spread of enlightenment among them, that by diffusion of education, they become better subjects and public servants' (Vijayanand, 1995; p. 17). This was the first policy statement on education. One and a half centuries later, in 1991, Kerala became a totally literate[1] state, where the state plays a significant role in the education sector.

Kerala now has a good infrastructure for education, especially for schools. As of 1995, Kerala had 12,092 schools, of which 4,455 (36.83%) are government schools, 7,297 private, but government-aided schools (60.37%); and 342 schools (2.83%) are private unaided schools. The role of the private sector in the Indian educational system is different from that of other countries. Private schools in India can be classified into government-aided and non-aided (self financing). For aided private schools, more than 95% of the recurring expenditure and some part of capital expenditure are met by the government. 97.13% of the schools in Kerala are run with government finance.[2] While in some of the other

Indian states, a disproportionately higher share goes to private aided schools at the cost of expenses on government schools, in Kerala, government assistance to the private sector as a percentage of total government expenditure at a given level of education is reasonable (Tilak, 1995).

The state school infrastructure consists of 6,694 primary schools, 2,520 government upper primary schools, 4,041 private aided schools and 133 unaided schools. In addition, there are 613 high schools having lower primary sections, 1,981 high schools with upper primary sections and 2,243 upper primary schools with lower primary sections. Government teachers constitute 36.8%, government-aided private schoolteachers, 60% and private unaided schoolteachers, 3.2%.

In 1994–95, 96.84% students were enrolled in government and government-aided private schools, while only 3.15% were enrolled in private unaided schools. Of the general population, 37.77% are in government schools, 59.09% in government-aided private schools and 3.15% in private unaided schools. Of the oppressed classes, 43.23% of SC students, and 55.25% of the ST students are in government schools, 55.94% of SC and 43.96% of the ST students are in government-aided private schools and 0.82% and 0.78% of the SC and ST students respectively, are in private unaided schools.

The proportion of educational expenditure to the total budget of the states over the years shows that Kerala had been spending a considerable percentage on education – much more than the national average and more than other states (except in 1992–93, when West Bengal took over the lead).

Furthermore, in comparison with all India average and other states, Kerala had been spending more of its income on education, as a proportion of its state domestic product (Table 3.1).

Table 3.1 Private aided schools as percentage of total* schools and the percentage of government expenditure during 1986–87

States	Primary	Government assistance	Secondary	Government assistance	Higher secondary	Government assistance
Andhra Pradesh	4.5	7.2	8.0	19.0	12.3	24.6
Assam	0.1	7.7	7.2	49.2	32.7	65.8
Bihar	1.1	1.4	3.0	6.2	5.2	0.0
Gujarat	1.5	0.0	6.9	87.5	92.7	60.1
Haryana	1.2	1.2	2.3	3.5	12.8	25.6
Karnataka	1.3	9.7	9.5	51.1	59.5	33.1
Kerala	59.9	55.3	66.6	53.4	59.5	70.2
Madhya Pradesh	1.9	3.3	3.9	11.8	12.4	14.4
Maharashtra	3.6	0.1	3.9	85.7	84.5	53.3
Orissa	3.0	18.7	93.7	68.1	79.9	26.7
Punjab	0.5	1.0	2.8	11.8	12.8	28.8
Rajasthan	1.3	2.5	3.7	5.0	4.7	11.6

States	Primary	Government assistance	Secondary	Government assistance	Higher secondary	Government assistance
Tamil Nadu	17.3	25.8	34.7	33.3	19.8	28.0
Uttar Pradesh	1.0	89.6	14.9	79.3	76.7	68.8
West Bengal	10.8	43.9	99.7	90.4	99.4	52.9
All India	4.5	21.5	17.8	48.2	15.3	37.1

Key: * total denotes the total of all government and private aided schools in the state.
Source: Tilak, 1995.

Table 3.2   Proportion of educational expenditure to total budget of the states (Revenue account only) (in %)

States	1965–66	1970–71	1975–76	1980–81	1985–86	1990–91	1992–93
Andhra Pradesh	20.4	20.9	27.0	25.7	25.6	24.5	19.6
Assam	21.1	20.8	26.8	29.0	23.1	25.5	24.7
Bihar	17.2	19.5	29.9	26.5	27.9	28.1	21.2
Gujarat	19.9	20.2	25.9	23.6	28.3	24.3	19.1

States	1965–66	1970–71	1975–76	1980–81	1985–86	1990–91	1992–93
Haryana	–	19.8	20.0	21.2	22.3	18.6	15.9
Karnataka	23.4	21.3	24.6	22.3	22.0	22.1	20.8
Kerala	36.0	35.7	39.7	35.5	31.7	30.4	26.2
Madhya Pradesh	25.6	24.2	21.7	21.4	21.0	24.2	17.8
Maharashtra	22.5	21.3	24.7	24.0	22.4	21.1	17.7
Orissa	13.4	16.8	24.0	22.8	22.2	24.2	19.4
Punjab	29.2	22.1	26.2	29.3	23.9	22.7	17.8
Rajasthan	19.8	18.9	24.7	26.0	26.4	26.5	21.5
Tamil Nadu	24.3	22.5	23.6	24.3	27.4	23.7	20.3
Uttar Pradesh	20.4	18.2	29.9	22.0	21.8	24.0	18.1
West Bengal	18.5	23.0	24.9	24.2	25.8	30.4	27.5
All India	21.3	21.4	25.8	23.8	24.0	25.4	20.0

Source: Tilak, 1995.

Table 3.3   Expenditure on education as a proportion of SDP for major Indian states (selected years)

States	1980–81	1990–91
Andhra Pradesh	3.8	4.6
Assam	3.6	6.0
Bihar	3.6	6.3
Gujarat	3.5	4.3
Haryana	2.7	3.1
Karnataka	3.4	4.3
Kerala	5.7	6.5
Madhya Pradesh	5.3	5.0
Maharashtra	3.5	5.4
Orissa	3.8	3.5
Punjab	3.5	5.3
Rajasthan	3.7	5.0
Tamil Nadu	4.3	11.8
Uttar Pradesh	3.1	4.6
West Bengal	2.9	5.4
All-India average	3.0	4.9

In Kerala, primary education is given priority. Of the total estimated expenditure of 13.78 billion rupees during 1994–95, 46.88% was spent on primary education, 31.6% on secondary education and 16.78% on university and higher education. Expenditure on education since 1989–90 and the cost of school education per pupil are given in tables.

Table 3.4   Expenditure on education in Kerala for selected years (Rupees in millions)

Stage	1989–90	1991–92	1993–94
Primary education	3,051.70	4,990.00	5,304.60
Secondary education	1,822.30	2,420.00	3,391.00
University education	832.10	1,220.00	2,148.20
Adult education	23.00	3.20	16.00
Language development	31.60	39.10	48.60
Technical education	276.20	380.00	592.50
Total	6,036.90	8,152.30	11,500.90

Table 3.5 Cost of school education in Kerala per pupil per annum – selected years (in Rupees)

Year	Primary	Secondary
1989–90	690.12	1,248.15
1991–92	953.48	1,600.00
1993–94	1,265.41	2,098.39

Source: *Economic Review*, 1995.

The state government expenditure on education for the past one decade came to more than 40% of the developmental expenditure.

Provision of health care

Accessibility has been a key factor in government intervention in health care provision in Kerala. According to 1993 data, there is one sub-centre for every 4,565 persons and one primary health centre for a population of 25,520 in Kerala. On an average, there are four sub-centres for every village and two primary health centres for every three villages in Kerala. The maximum radial distance covered by a sub-centre in Kerala is 1.85 km against 2.76 at all India level and a primary health centre 3.95 km against all India figure of 6.73 km. The high density of population and better transport system enables easy access to medicare in Kerala. Over the years, health care institutions like hospitals, dispensaries, primary health centres, maternity and child health centres have not only grown in number but also spread widely over the state. The easy accessibility has benefited poor sections, considering the opportunity cost.

In 1995, the health care infrastructure consists of 147 hospitals (5 general hospitals, 11 district hospitals, 36 taluk[3] hospitals, 73 intermediate hospitals, 8 women and children's hospitals, 5 medical college hospitals and 3 mental hospitals, 3 leprosy hospitals, 3 TB hospitals).

In respect of population-bed ratio, Kerala has the most beds per population in India. Furthermore, unlike other parts of India, where only less than 20% of the facilities are in rural areas (for a population who form nearly 80% of the total population), bed facilities are spread over both urban and rural Kerala. Including the grant-in-aid institutions, there are 1,263 allopathic medical institutions, with a total bed strength of 42,216.

When we take into account the 108 ayurveda hospitals, with 2,329 beds and 31 homeopathy hospitals, with 950 beds, there is 1 bed per 676 population (When hospitals under private and co-operative sectors are also taken into account, there is 1 bed per 250 population).

Krishnan (Sadanandan, 1993; p. 13) highlights the role of state intervention in health care, especially, in immunisation services; as the major cause for decline of mortality rates in Kerala. Nag (1983), comparing West Bengal and Kerala, attributes the role of government in prevention-oriented wide coverage as the reason for better health status in Kerala.

Expenditure on health

Total expenditure on medical and public health and per capita expenditure have been going up steadily in Kerala. The government is spending 3,992.77 million rupees on health including family welfare. Over the past decade, the per capita expenditure has more than doubled.

At the same time, Kerala is losing its lead on per capita health care expenditure (Reddy and Selvaraju, 1994). In 1974–75, Kerala had the first rank, with a per capita expenditure of Rs. 50.36, in 1978–79, Kerala's rank was fourth and the per capita expenditure was Rs. 39.67; in 1982–83, the rank was second, and the expenditure was Rs. 57.28 per capita, in 1986–87 and 1990–91, Kerala stood second, spending Rs. 69.59 and Rs. 73.66 respectively.

Family welfare programmes

Family welfare programmes in Kerala are implemented through a network of 940 primary health centres and 5,094 sub centres. The programme broadly consists of family welfare programmes for family planning, Mother and Health programmes concentrating on immunisation against DPT, polio, BCG, meals, TT for pregnant women, etc. The family planning achievements for the last four years are given in Table 3.6.

In Kerala, vaccine preventable diseases (VPD) are under control, due to the immunization programme known as the Expanded Programme on Immunization, started in 1978. In another programme called Universal Immunization Programme (UIP), launched in 1988, all the districts are covered. Kerala is the first state in India where all districts are covered under UIP (Rajmohanan, 1994).

Table 3.6   Achievements in family planning – selected years (in numbers)

	1992	1993	1994	1995
Sterilisation	173,599	159,823	131,173	41,555
Intrauterine contraceptive users	115,446	101,170	84,854	87,711
Contraceptive users	296,359	288,370	257,169	297,969
Oral contraceptive users	38,970	33,896	32,493	39,935

Reducing regional disparities

Kerala's social development process shows that regional disparities can be overcome within a single generation. The three regions – Travancore, Cochin and Malabar – which joined to form 'United Kerala'; had significant differences in the levels of social development. As Nossiter (1982) rightly points out, 'Malabar was a neglected outpost of Madras, on which the British spent little beyond the requirement of law and order' (p. 15). On the other hand, the Travancore and Cochin governments (more so, Travancore) consistently pursued development activities which resulted in better social indicators. During the time of 'integration' Malabar was the least developed of the three states. Though northern Keralites, of the erstwhile Malabar still cry discrimination, and disparities still remain, the level of inter-regional differences has been considerably reduced. What the rest of Kerala has achieved during the span of a century, Malabar has achieved in less than four decades. This leads us to the role of government intervention in sustaining and improving social development and raising the level of social development in a region which was clearly lagging behind.

In 1955–56, Malabar had only 90 primary, 25 middle and 11 secondary schools, but in 1960–61, the numbers increased to 1,083, 248 and 100 respectively. In 1990–91, Malabar had a total of 5,477 schools of which 1,866 were government schools. In 1955–56, before the integration, the number of government schools in Malabar was just 130.

Table 3.7   Government intervention in reduction of regional disparity – education sector

Year	Travancore–Cochin region		Malabar region	
	Total no. of schools	Percentage of government schools	Total no. of schools	Percentage of government schools
1950–51	4,249	43.56	4,282	3.04
1955–56	4,666	40.87	4,669	2.70
1960–61	5,264	38.24	4,524	31.63
1965–66	5,684	43.07	4,905	32.40
1980–81	6,274	39.85	5,236	34.15
1985–86	6,672	39.22	5,464	33.93
1990–91	6,656	39.66	5,477	34.07

Source: Compiled from various records of the education department, Kerala.

While Travancore and Cochin were spending about 5% of their revenue on health, Malabar district was utilising only 2% of the total revenue on health. This was reflected in health indicators, with Malabar lagging far behind Travancore and Cochin regions, for example, death rates. Though the death rate for Malabar is not available, the death rate for Travancore–Cochin in 1941 was 14.6, and for United Kerala (including Travancore, Cochin and Malabar) during 1941–50 22.3 (a rate higher than Travancore and Cochin). Panikar and Soman (1984) observe that 'this would imply a higher mortality in the Malabar districts'. Since the formation of United Kerala, the state as a whole shows a much lower average death rate. This proves that there has been considerable improvement in the medicare facilities in the (erstwhile) Malabar region and that inter-regional disparities have been sharply reduced. The considerable improvement in the population-bed ratio of the Northern region is a case in point. In 1956–57, Malabar had a population-bed ratio of 3,125 compared to 1,282 persons in Travancore–Cochin. In 1989–90, the corresponding figures were 1,021 and 642 respectively. This has resulted in the reduction of both the infrastructural and the utilisation gap between north and south regions of Kerala. For example, 84% of the births in Malabar were under medical supervision, against 98% in the Travancore–Cochin region. Though slight disparities exist, there has been considerable improvement in health care infrastructure in the northern region, with the result that the infant mortality rates in the two regions are almost identical.

Provision of food security

Public Distribution System (PDS)

Due to historical and climatic factors, Kerala has developed commercial agriculture more than food crops. Consequently the state is short of food grains, especially rice, the staple of the people. In 1994–95, out of a gross cropped area of 3.04 million hectares (ha.), the share of food crops (rice, pulses, millets and tapioca) occupied only 22 per cent. The gap between the demand and supply of food grains which was around 50 per cent in the mid seventies has started widening due to large scale shift in paddy lands to cash crops (*Economic Review*, 1995).

For a food-deficit state like Kerala, specializing in non-food crops, the role of an effective PDS is very important. Apart from ensuring supply of essential commodities at reasonable prices, PDS helps in stabilizing market prices.

The PDS in Kerala, the best among Indian states, provides basic nutritional support to its people. While PDS in most of the other States is limited to urban areas, the coverage in Kerala is total, through a well designed network of ration shops. In 1991, the average amount of food-grain bought from ration shops by an individual in Kerala was 69.6 kg. The corresponding figures for Uttar Pradesh and Bihar in 1989 were 6 kg and 8 kg respectively (Ramachandran, 1995). All sections[4] of the society, especially the weaker and vulnerable sections of Kerala, benefit from the

PDS. The open market price of essential food grains has always been higher than the ration prices.[5]

The PDS in Kerala has its roots in the statutory rationing of the Second World War period in Cochin, when government intervened to make up for the stoppage of rice imports from Burma (Vijayanand 1995). PDS in the state was introduced under the provisions of the Essential Commodities Act 1955, through the Kerala Rationing Order 1966. The government of India allots the ration items one month in advance for distribution. More than 14,000 ration shops distribute these ration items – rice, wheat, sugar, palm oil and kerosene to 5,650,000 households. The coverage is more than 90 per cent of the households in the state. Nearly 2/3rd of the cereal purchase of poorer households are met through the PDS. This is the highest in the country. On an average, there is one outlet for every 405 card holders covering a population of 28.34 million with 22.81 million adults and 5.53 million non-adults.

Apart from ration shops, the state has another distribution network of 3,161 outlets selling pulses, spices etc. at reasonable prices.

Supplementary nutrition programmes

The nutrition programmes implemented in the state are the Integrated Child Development Service (ICDS), the Special Nutrition Programme in Urban Areas (SNP), both under the Social Welfare Department, the Composite Programme for Women and Pre-school children (CPWC), under the Rural Development Department and the School Meals Programme, implemented by Education Dept.

Though these programmes have been in existence for more than two decades, the coverage of the SNP gained momentum only from the early 1980s. The objective of this programme is to combat malnutrition by providing 300 calories and 15 gms of protein for pregnant and nursing mothers for 300 days a year. This programme is managed through a network of 16,209 (as of 1995) 'anganwadis', managed by educated women.

ICDS is a package programme for feeding, immunization, nutrition, health care, referral services, nutrition education and pre-school education. Applied Nutritional Programme (ANP) helps women to develop kitchen gardens, and prepare nutritious foods with locally available materials.

Table 3.8   Public distribution of essential commodities in Kerala

Year	Rice ('000 metric tonnes)	Wheat	Sugar ('000 KL)	Kerosene ('000 MT)	Palmoil	Cloth Std. bales ('000)	Shops	Families millions
1975	531	490	-	-	-	-	1.14	3.62
1976	904	220	-	-	-	-	1.16	3.87
1977	1,363	65	-	-	-	-	1.18	4.03
1978	896	36	-	-	-	-	1.19	4.04
1979	549	33	-	-	-	-	1.18	4.05
1980	770	48	126	167	-	13,806	1.09	4.05
1981	1,063	44	123	178	-	8,698	1.15	4.10
1982	1,159	59	126	190	-	3,646	1.15	4.11
1983	1,288	202	150	208	37	6,101	1.19	4.19
1984	1,325	147	127	222	48	5,573	1.22	4.30
1985	1,384	110	142	235	43	3,833	1.25	4.37
1986	1,560	98	140	258	-	6,714	1.26	4.48

Year	Rice	Wheat ('000 metric tonnes)	Sugar ('000 KL)	Kerosene ('000 MT)	Palmoil ('000 MT)	Cloth Std. bales ('000)	Shops	Families millions
1987	1,598	104	146	292	43	9,166	1.28	4.73
1988	1,546	150	141	3,088	64	-	1.28	4.81
1989	1,270	209	148	322	31	-	1.29	4.91
1990	1,649	232	151	338	71	-	1.30	5.00
1991	1,671	333	145	334	29	-	1.30	5.06

Source: Kannan, 1995.

The school mid-day programme feeds school going children in class I to IV (and class V, if it is attached to the primary school). CARE extended full commodity support from 1961 to 1970 and partial support till mid 80s. Now the programme is run with the support and financial assistance of the state government. The objective of the scheme is to provide approximately 410 calories and 15 gms of protein. The state government supplies commodities, a part time person cooks and the programme is managed at local level by the school Parent-Teachers Association.

Table 3.9   Beneficiaries of school meal programme – selected years

Year	Total no. of pupils in millions (Class I to IV)	No. of beneficiaries (millions)	Percentage
1970–71	2.87	2.08	73
1980–81	2.60	1.78	67
1990–91	2.47	1.38	56

Source: Kannan, *Economic and Political Weekly*, 14–21 October 1995.

Kannan (1995) has estimated that the Special Meal Programme benefited the rural labour households by Rs. 120 in 1983–84 and Rs. 139 in 1986–87. The money equivalent of supplementary nutrition programmes comes to Rs. 102 in 1983–84 and Rs. 100 in 1986–87.

Table 3.10 shows the list of projects, number of centres and number of beneficiaries for selected years.

Provision of Social Security

Social security in Kerala broadly comprises three dimensions of intervention – pensions, welfare assistance and institutional care. In Kerala, social security is perceived as an entitlement of the poor and disabled. It is aimed at people who are unable to participate in economic activities for reasons of old age and physical or mental disabilities or who have no other means of independent income. The government of Kerala (GOK) defines social security as 'the provision given by society through a series of measures to such members who are not in a position to support

Table 3.10   Supplementary nutrition and health programmes for women and children

Year	SNP		ICDS		ANP		CPWC	
	NC	NB	NC	NB	NC	NB	NC	NB
1979–80	1,750	0.30	1,154	0.09	-	-	-	-
1980–81	2,000	0.33	1,354	0.11	-	-	-	-
1981–82	4,029	0.52	2,029	0.19	-	-	-	-
1984–85	431	0.02	7,696	0.77	4,033	0.48	2,411	-
1985–86	472	0.03	8,100	0.78	2,213	0.11	1,798	0.14
1986–87	410	0.04	8,272	0.78	1,985	0.10	1,790	0.13
1987–88	470	0.04	9,227	0.78	1,705	0.09	1,652	0.13
1988–89	463	0.04	10,064	0.77	1,611	0.10	1,652	0.12
1989–90	459	0.04	9,651	0.66	1,611	0.10	1,550	0.12
1990–91	471	0.44	9,850	0.73	1,509	0.10	1,433	0.11

Keys: NC: Number of centres; NB: Number of beneficiaries in millions; SNP: Special Nutritional Programme; ICDS: Integrated Child Development Scheme.
Source: Kannan (1995).

themselves due to a variety of extraneous factors resulting from sickness, maternity, employment injury (including occupational disease), unemployment (including absence of employment) and under employment, invalidity, destitution, social disability and backwardness, old age and death etc.' (*Economic Review*, 1993).

Kerala has a proven record of wider commitment in social security measures for the benefit of the poor and under-privileged segments of society. The successive governments in Kerala have introduced several social security initiatives. During the period 1986 to 1991, the expenditure on social security and welfare measures came to about 3,700 million rupees.[6] From 1991 to 1994, the government spent 2,800 million rupees. During 1994–95 alone the expenditure was about 930 million rupees. For the last ten years from 1985, state government has been spending 40 per cent of the total state expenditure on social services.

Including the three major pension schemes, Kerala has more than 35 social security and welfare schemes covering about 3 million persons (*Economic Review*, 1995). The agricultural worker's pension scheme, destitute and widow pensions scheme and special pension for the physically handicapped benefited 0.6 million people in 1994. In the same year, 20.4 per cent of the total 60 plus population was covered under major pension schemes (*Economic Review*, 1994).

All these pension schemes are financed out of state funds. 12 per cent of the total households in Kerala availed of these pensions in 1991–92, against 5 per cent of households in the neighbouring state of Tamil Nadu (Gulati and Gulati, 1995). The coverage under major pension schemes with qualifying conditions and the amount of assistance are given in Table 3.11.

Provision of institutionalization

In Kerala, institutional care is ensured through '*abalamandirs*' (homes for the destitute), rescue homes, after care hostels, care hostels, orphanages, homes for the disabled, mentally retarded etc. As on 31.3.1995, institutionalized care is provided to more than 51,000 orphans. The details of major social security and welfare schemes implemented by the Social Welfare Department are given in Table 3.12.

Table 3.11   Major pension schemes in Kerala

Name of scheme and year of starting	Qualifying condition and Present rate of assistance[7]	Beneficiaries
Agricultural Workers Pension Scheme (1980)	Eligible age, above 60. Annual family income not to exceed Rs. 15,000. Rs. 100 per month	344,946
Kerala Destitute Pension Scheme (1960)	Above 65 years of age. For widowed destitute no age limit. Annual income not to exceed Rs. 1,200. Rs. 100 per month	1,892,263
Special Pension scheme for the Physically Handicapped, Disabled and Mentally Retarded Person (1982)	Pension for people with minimum 40 per cent disability. Beneficiaries monthly income not to exceed Rs. 75 and family income not to exceed Rs. 5,000. Rs. 100 per month	90,906
Kerala Freedom Fighters pension scheme (1971)	Rs. 500 per month	12,000
Pension to sportsmen (1977)	Income limit Rs. 11,000 per year. 55–60 years, Rs. 200 per month; 60–70 years, Rs. 300; 70 and above, Rs. 400	157

Table 3.12 **Major social security and welfare schemes implemented by the Social Welfare Department (1994–95)**

Name of scheme and year of starting	Nature of care	No. of persons benefited
Abalamandir (Shelter for waifs and strays) (1961)	Welfare of the destitute girls and women	125
Govt. Balasadhan	Welfare of children, orphans etc.	100
Rescue Homes	Detention of the women girls under the provision of Suppression of Immoral Traffic in Women and Girls Act	100
After-care hostels (for women)	-do-	50
Care Homes	Welfare and Rehabilitation of the old age and Ex-convicts	100
Home for mentally deficient children	Give care and special training to mentally deficient children	100
Care home for disabled children	Giving protection to the disabled children up to the age of 16	75
Home for Physically Handicapped	For the welfare of the physically handicapped men, women, old and inform	225
Children's Home	For the welfare of leper patients' children	50
Home for the cured mental patients	For the accommodation and rehabilitation of the cured mental patients	50

Provision of security through welfare funds

Several welfare fund schemes initiated by the state government provide security to employees/workers in the organized and unorganized sectors. Today there are more than a dozen welfare fund schemes for different type of workers such as Toddy workers[8], Head load workers[9], motor transport workers, etc.

The objectives of these Welfare Funds are to provide welfare assistance during their course of labour participation and economic security during the retirement phase. The fund constitutes contribution from the employers, employees and in some cases, by the government. Employer's contribution towards the fund is more than that of the workers. Major welfare fund schemes, beneficiaries, estimated no. of workers covered/benefited, amount spent during 1994–95 are given in Table 3.13.

Table 3.13 Major welfare fund schemes in Kerala

Name of the scheme	Beneficiaries (in 1,000s)	Amount spent[b]
Kerala Toddy[a] Workers Welfare Fund Scheme, 1969	43	14.62
Kerala Headload Workers (Regulation of Employment and Welfare) Scheme, 1983	200	0.67
Kerala Motor Transport Workers Welfare Fund Scheme, 1986	32	6.30
Kerala Fishermen Welfare Fund Scheme, 1986	162	6.30
Kerala Artisans and Skilled Workers Death-cum-Retirement Benefit Scheme, 1986	n.a.	27.90
Kerala Cashew Workers Welfare Fund, 1988	150	8.86
Kerala Coir Workers Welfare Fund Scheme, 1989	350	9.20
Kerala Handloom Workers Welfare Fund Scheme, 1989	250	n.a.
Kerala Construction Workers Welfare Fund, 1990	1,000	14.07
Kerala Abkari Workers Welfare Fund, 1990	75	0.47

Keys: [a] Country liquor; [b] during 1994–95; Rupees in million.

Provision of security to other vulnerable groups

Apart from those mentioned above, there are three major schemes for the most vulnerable sections of society.

1.　Financial assistance to leprosy and cancer patients: On the basis of a certificate from hospital and subject to an income ceiling of Rs. 200 per month, leprosy and cancer patients are given Rs. 100 per month. During 1994–95, the state spent 3.18 million rupees and 5,300 patients benefited. The scheme came into force in 1976.
2.　Financial assistance to widows: This scheme was introduced in 1978. Under the scheme, a consolidated amount of Rs. 1,000 is given to the widows for marriage of their daughters. For eligibility, there is an income ceiling of Rs. 5,000 per year. In 1993–94, 8,800 widows were given financial assistance.
3.　Accident insurance scheme for students: 5,717,000 students were covered under this scheme in 1994–95. The premium is paid by the state government and the cover includes Rs. 10,000 for death or total disability due to accident. Partial disability, minor injuries are also covered under this scheme, which came into force in 1989.

Provision of social security to the unemployed

Table 3.14　Unemployment assistance in Kerala

Year	No. of beneficiaries	Amount disbursed (Rupees in millions)
1985–86	179,146	101.21
1986–87	218,446	83.50
1987–88	205,556	109.57
1988–89	215,456	235.38
1989–90	246,040	199.64
1990–91	264,314	193.49
1991–92	260,196	161.96
1992–93	229,143	62.57
1993–94	273,512	174.87
1994–95	269,683	142.68

Source: *Economic Review*, 1995.

The unemployment situation being so severe in Kerala, the state government has had a scheme for the unemployed since 1981. As per this scheme, financial assistance of Rs. 70 per month is given to those who wait for employment in the live register of the Employment Exchange for more than three years. Table 3.14 shows the number of beneficiaries and the total amount spent every year for the past 10 years.

Provision of welfare and security to the oppressed classes

There are numerous schemes exclusively for the social and economic development of scheduled castes and scheduled tribes. Though the majority of the welfare programmes for SC and ST are implemented through scheduled castes and scheduled tribes departments, sectoral departments are also implementing schemes for overall development of these oppressed classes of Kerala society.

Scheduled castes

The special component plan is a major scheme for improving living conditions of the scheduled castes population. A percentage of funds from sectoral departments are utilised for the provision of drinking water, roads, houses, educational and health facilities, electrification etc.

Under the scheduled castes development department, there are 76 '*balawadis*' (kindergartens) and feeding centres, 53 boys' hostels, 48 girls' hostels, 788 other institutions, 41 industrial training centres, 3 production cum training centres, 3 pre-examination training centres and one I.A.S. (Indian Administrative Service) coaching centre. There are about 44 programmes exclusively for scheduled castes. These include provisions for scholarships to students, adult education, interest free housing loans, thatching and tiling grants, housing grants, assistance for marriage and treatment of major illnesses like cancer, seasonal day care centres for the children of women labourers, interest free industrial loans, so on and so forth.

Scheduled tribes

Like the scheduled castes development department, the scheduled tribe development department is also implementing various schemes. In the education sector, apart from providing scholarships, stipends and other incentives, the department also runs 115 hostels, 14 nursery schools and 30 infant care centres. In the area of housing, this department provides grants for building houses, rehabilitates landless and houseless families by purchasing land and building for them. Members of scheduled tribes are given industrial loans and housing loans. In the area of health, this department runs hospitals, dispensaries, midwifery centres and mobile medical units. The department also has schemes for treatment and rehabilitation of tribals affected by tuberculosis, leprosy and other diseases.

Social expenditure in Kerala

In the last chapter we have statistically established that Kerala's achievements in the physical qualities of life exceeds that predicted by its SDP. On a comparison with other Indian states, we found that Kerala has the highest and most significant positive value of economic development–social development disparity.

Table 3.15   Per capita social expenditure of major Indian states during 1990–91*

States	Social expenditure	Educational expenditure	Medical expenditure	Total social development expenditure
Andhra Pradesh	175.94	82.71	33.68	292.33
Assam	184.53	106.46	45.96	336.95
Bihar	119.02	72.2	24.34	215.56
Gujarat	215.23	113.89	42.53	371.65
Haryana	218.23	106.56	43.39	368.18
Karnataka	188.33	94.12	37.27	319.72
Kerala	227.23	131.27	49.09	407.59

States	Social expenditure	Educational expenditure	Medical expenditure	Total social development expenditure
Madhya Pradesh	151.37	70.95	34.61	256.93
Maharashtra	216.62	117.08	45.37	379.07
Orissa	156.55	78.86	33.74	269.15
Punjab	250.27	144.01	57.64	451.92
Rajasthan	181.59	94.18	60.04	335.81
Tamil Nadu	234.3	112.72	50.29	397.31
Uttar Pradesh	125.32	74.68	29.39	229.39
West Bengal	166.09	92.05	36.32	294.46

Key: * at 1982–83 prices.
Source: *Economic and Political Weekly*, 21 May 1994; p. 1308.

To understand the role and contribution of government in attaining PQLI, in this section we will analyze the social sector spending of major state governments in India. The fundamental question in government expenditure on the social sector is how far it is influenced by the income of the state government. Is Kerala spending more on social sectors than would be expected of its SDP. We have combined the social health and education expenses of state governments to arrive at the social spending.

Statistical analysis

A linear function is chosen relating total social development expenditure (Y) to per capita SDP (X).

$$Y = a + bX$$

where 'a' is the intercept and 'b' the slope and is estimated with ordinary least squares. Parameter estimates for equation (1) are given in equation (2) with 't' values indicated in parenthesis.

$$R^2 = 0.567382$$
$$Y = 174.0074 + 0.031367X$$
$$(4.427236) \ (4.129114)$$

**Table 3.16   Values of economic development – social development
               expenditure disparity**

States	Social development expenditure			Remarks
	Actual	Predicted	Residuals	
Andhra Pradesh	292.33	322.3099	–29.9799	
Assam	336.95	299.914	37.03605	
Bihar	215.56	257.2864	–41.7264	
Gujarat	371.65	352.3907	19.25929	
Haryana	368.18	409.3216	–41.1416	
Karnataka	319.72	321.3062	–1.58615	
Kerala	**407.59**	**305.9678**	**101.6222**	**significant at 2 std. deviation**
Madhya Pradesh	256.93	304.1485	–47.2185	significant at 1 std. deviation
Maharashtra	379.07	403.4873	–24.4173	
Orissa	269.15	270.5232	–1.37321	
Punjab	451.92	436.6421	15.27791	
Rajasthan	335.81	303.0193	32.79073	
Tamil Nadu	397.31	332.3159	64.99408	significant at 1 std. deviation
Uttar Pradesh	229.39	284.2933	–54.9033	significant at 1 std. deviation
West Bengal	294.46	323.0941	–28.6341	

Kerala, whose social development expenditure far exceeds the expected
(i.e., social development expenditure is greater than that predicted by
SDP), has a positive value of disparity measure. In the last chapter, it was
proved that Kerala has been successful in converting economic resources
to social development. It is clear from the statistical analysis that by
incurring a higher social development expenditure than is expected of its
SDP, the state has played a significant role in attaining a high physical
quality of life for its population. The disparity measure for Kerala is highly
significant at 2 standard deviations. Tamil Nadu, the only other state with
positive correlation (at 1 standard deviation) has considerably improved its
rank among major Indian states in social expenditure over the last two

decades. In 1975–76, Tamil Nadu had the fifth rank in social expenditure, sixth rank in educational expenditure and seventh rank in expenditure on medical, public health etc. In 1990–91, in social expenditure it stood second, in educational expenditure fourth and medical and public health second. In fact, in evaluating the inter-state disparities, EPW Research Foundation found the performance of Tamil Nadu (along with Kerala) commendable in literacy achievements, especially for women, demographic development and reducing rural-urban disparities in crude birth rates and death rates.

Conclusion

In this chapter we found that the state government has played, and is playing a crucial role in the social sectors. The education policies of the state government have led to total literacy and near-universalisation of education. Apart from setting up of schools, the state government is aiding private schools. The state is spending a considerable percentage of its revenue on education, especially on primary education. Even the World Bank (1995), along with its prescriptions for state withdrawal in India, gives much emphasis to the role of state in delivering primary education. The health care policies of the government have ensured better health care facilities. The government of Kerala has made inroads into primary health care and the relatively better health indicators of Kerala could be attributed to the high expenditure on health and family welfare programmes. Both the education and health policies empowered people in Kerala to avail themselves of health care facilities. The state government has been successful in reducing the inter-regional differences between Malabar and Travancore–Cochin, within a span of four decades. The public distribution system ensures freedom from hunger at low cost. Unlike other Indian states, the PDS in Kerala is universal and free from urban bias.

The state has several nutrition schemes and has been successful in providing social security provision to workers from unorganized sector and vulnerable groups like widows. It is noteworthy that Kerala has been a leader among the Indian states in providing welfare fund schemes.

In the previous chapter, we found that Kerala has achieved higher PQLI than that would be expected of its SDP and in this chapter we found that Kerala had been spending higher amounts on the social sectors than would be expected of its SDP. Thus it could be concluded that the higher PQLI than which would be expected of its SDP was to a considerable extent, a result of higher social expenditure.

This chapter is based on government statistics giving a comparative perspective on other Indian states. The quality of services in the social sector has not been discussed. It is nearly impossible to get information on the quality of social services in the major Indian states. Nor does the analysis imply that the social security provisions in Kerala are adequate. The widow's pension of Rs. 100, for example, will not take care of even the basic needs of an individual, let alone of a family. At the same time, the social security provisions in Kerala are more than those in the other Indian states. The social assistance schemes and welfare measures provide security to the vulnerable sections of society. Having statistically established the contribution of state government towards high physical quality of life at the macro-level, let us examine how government officials perceive the development processes in Kerala.

Notes

1   Total literacy is functional literacy, which, according to National Literacy Mission (India), involves, among other social skills, the ability to read, write and acquire basic numeracy skills.
2   Government spends money on both government schools and private-aided schools.
3   Districts are further divided into taluks.
4   90% of the population hold ration cards, which entitles them to buy subsidized rice, wheat, sugar, cooking oil, kerosene and cloth from the ration shops.
5   For example, in the summer of 1995, the retail price of one kg of rice in the open market was above Rs. 10, while the ration price was Rs. 7.
6   We have not been successful in finding the corresponding figures for other Indian states.
7   The value of 1 US$ varies from Rs. 40 to Rs. 44/-. In December 1999, one kg. rice, costs Rs. 13/- one kg. of dry chillies, Rs. 70/- 1 litre of milk Rs. 13/-; 1 kg. of coconut oil, Rs. 70/- . These are approximate figures and the list is only indicative.
8   Workers engaged in production and distribution of *kallu*, country liquor, fermented from the sap of coconut palm.
9   Workers who carry heavy loads on their heads.

4 Development in Kerala: Perceptions of Government Officials

The previous chapters shed light on the complexities of Kerala's development pattern. On a macro-level analysis based on social indicators, we found that Kerala has achieved higher physical quality of life, than would be expected based on its SDP and that Kerala government's expenditure on social sectors, is more than would be expected of its SDP. Public action and government intervention have been identified as the reasons for better quality of life of people in Kerala.

This chapter is based on extensive interviews conducted by Sundar Ramanathaiyer, with eight senior development officials from different state government departments in Kerala in the summer of 1995. The social development pursuits of the state are implemented through government officials. Hence their perceptions and experiences with the social development process, the role and contribution of government and the problems with conceptualization and implementation of welfare schemes, are very important. In a democratic set-up, although politicians are mainly responsible for evolving social development directions, the role of the bureaucracy cannot be underestimated. Bureaucracy may not really affect the manner in which legislative assembly members get elected, but they do influence and contribute to the policy agenda. Gulati (1995) argues that only when the bureaucrat prepares projects, will the politicians be aware of their feasibility. An efficient bureaucracy can guide and advise the ministry. So far, no attempt has been made to understand administrators' perceptions and experiences with the social development process in Kerala. What follows is an attempt in that direction.

The officials were asked about their perceptions of the factors that played a significant role in social development processes in Kerala; about the groups left out in the process and the approaches of bureaucracy to social development. They were also asked about the government policies

82

and schemes and the bottlenecks in their implementation. The role of women in development, the impact of new economic reforms of the central government and perceptions on the future of social development in Kerala, were the other topics discussed during the interviews.

Before presenting the material, we will introduce the officials who kindly agreed to be interviewed. Kerala has state government departments for public health, development, education, industries, agriculture, fisheries, social welfare, labour, along with departments exclusively for the welfare of scheduled castes and scheduled tribes. This list is not exhaustive, but represents the major departments engaged in social sectors. In most of the departments, officials can be transferred from one district to another and from one department to another within the secretariat in the state capital.

In India, social development activity by a state or central government is a complex process spreading over several departments. Hence officials to be interviewed were selected from various departments and their brief profiles are given below.

1. Mr. Appu, I.A.S. (a member of the Indian Administrative Service), is working as a senior executive in the health department. His contributions in introducing administrative reforms at the district level have been widely acknowledged.
2. Dr. Anand, a senior official in the health department, is a specialist in public health.
3. Dr. Nair, a sociologist, is from Kerala Water Authority, a department engaged in water supply and the provision of sanitation.
4. Dr. Arjun, I.A.S., an economist, has created an impact in Kerala government service by introducing new management techniques.
5. Mr. Menon, I.A.S., still known as the 'People's Collector', despite having left district administration in the mid-eighties, represents the tribal development department.
6. Mr. Ramu, I.A.S., from the education department, is best known for his 'sense of fairness' and 'conflicts with ministers'.
7. Mr. Bose, a senior official from the fisheries department, who, apart from being a marine scientist, has also been involved in several 'people oriented' schemes and projects for the fisherfolk.

8.   Mr. Kannan, who has been recognized and honoured by the President of India, for his social development pursuits, represents the rural development department.

These officials were selected after making detailed enquiries into their backgrounds. Only officials who are known to have contributed to social development in Kerala were selected. The prime parameters of selection were contributions to society and personal integrity. These officials represent the cream of Kerala bureaucracy. What follows is an honest expression of their attitudes and experiences. Often times they tended to be self-critical and introspective. One could feel anger, disillusionment, hope and concern in their voices.

Three officials insisted that their identity should not be revealed under any circumstance, while two others preferred anonymity. Hence all the names used in the chapter are pseudonyms, while the names of the departments and places are true.

All interviews, except one were recorded in Malayalam and took place at the respondents' homes. Only some portions of the interviews, which lasted between one to four hours, were transcribed and translated for use in this chapter. Wherever portions from the interviews are quoted, we have attempted to retain the informal and colloquial nature of the interviews.

On social development and its evolution in Kerala

To Ramu, Kerala has been very successful in ensuring high physical quality of life for its people and 'if we exclude Kerala and count the national PQLI or HDI, India's figures will go down'.

Ramu attributes three main factors to the high physical quality of life in Kerala. First there was the contribution of Maharajas. 'In no other Indian state have the Maharajas done so much for their people. They started schools and hospitals'. Then there was the contribution of Christian missionaries who dominated the field of private education before 1965. Later communal organizations founded educational institutions. Then during the 1930s to early sixties, the Communist party inculcated a consciousness of rights and empowerment into the poorer and weaker sections of the society. Ramu argues that a combination of these three factors – contributions of Maharajas toward education and health, the role of Christian missionaries in spreading education, and presence of a communist movement which made the weak and vulnerable sections of society aware of their rights – all contributed to the better standard of living in Kerala.

Menon contends that apart from the contribution of Maharajas to the process of development, Kerala's social development evolved out of an historical process of people's movement and a compressed period of deliberate governmental activity. This lasted probably till the mid-seventies and he feels that it is very difficult to prove whether there has been conscious deliberate action after that.

> There was a conscious process of social development from (the) mid-50s to (the) mid-70s. Because during the period of integration there was (a) considerable gap between Malabar and the rest of Kerala, (a) difference in the so-called indicators. With conscious effort, we were able to reduce that gap – mainly in education and health. That aspect is remarkable.

Arjun, in sharing his insights on social development in Kerala, is of the opinion that state intervention has its genesis in the socio-cultural environment prevalent in Kerala. The role of Christian missionaries and community based service organizations have reduced social inequalities to a large extent. He believes that 'organized state intervention at this stage had pre-empted a possible polarization on fundamentalist lines and has induced a balanced state wherein a healthy society could evolve'.

Kannan in contrast, firmly believes that the so-called Kerala model is the cumulative effect of a series of isolated interventions, a result of a lot of ad-hoc actions and not the result of a conscious effort in planning. 'A ministry introduces a few schemes. When that ministry changes, the new one announces a few other schemes and the process goes on. It's all ad-hoc action'.

Lack of a long-term perspective has affected what Menon calls 'planning the transitions'. He argues that every development effort result in 'some kind of transition'. He points out that demographic transition has led to the phenomenon of uneconomic schools. The reduction in birth rate would automatically affect the number of school-going children, after a lag. The need to cut down schools was not envisaged in the planning process. Again, having reached a comfortable position in literacy, 'we should have thought about converting that literacy into some form of skill'. One would ask whether children completing secondary school education, 'have or can they develop any skills that are essential in today's world?' The urgency with which Kerala executed educational and health campaigns is missing in vocational studies. The transitions have not made any impact on the planning processes.

> Kerala, for example, could have succeeded in software development. We have the orientation; we have the manpower and it doesn't require much in terms of infrastructure. Still we lost out. We argued that we are against computerization. By the time we started computer training courses, other states had already established a lead ... Logically, we should have been the first to accept computerisation.

Another result of demographic transition, the increasing number of elderly in the population and their needs; have not been planned for. Arjun says that 'elderly are not on the agenda now', while Appu says that 'much before government realized that this (care of the elderly) was a tremendous need, various social service agencies have taken it up in a large way'.

Anand argues that the governmental intervention in improving health and educational infrastructure was the result of 'locally raised demands, articulation of local demands and response of the institutions to those demands'. As to how that articulation originated, he says, it was very easy, because every village in Kerala 'had a certain critical mass of educated people; some of whom with real involvement in politics'. Enlightened people who were able to perceive people's needs joined political movements and articulated people's demands.

To him the government's response to Malabar's demands helped to narrow the gap between Malabar and Travancore–Cochin regions in provision of infrastructure such as hospitals, schools and roads.

> When Travancore–Cochin was amalgamated with Malabar, obviously Malabar people started articulating vociferously about the gap between Travancore–Cochin and Malabar. They were not satisfied with whatever each government was doing. From 1956 to 1980, *Mathrubhumi* and other newspapers were vocalizing the demands. When this demand was vocalized, obviously with the support of the members of the legislature, there was a lot of investment in Malabar, resulting in reduction of the gap.

Apart from the role and contribution of government in reducing the regional disparities, Anand attributes the inherent topography and the settlement pattern of Kerala as a major reason for improvement in health indices.

All the villages in Kerala are big and densely populated. Over 70 per cent of the villages have a population that is greater than 10,000. 'When the population is more than 10,000, it provides, for instance, an enormous opportunity (and) some sort of financial stability for the doctors, (who) can very well go and settle there. Ten thousand people means two thousand families and they can very well support a doctor'. Thus unlike the other Indian villages, the economies of scale became advantageous to Kerala.[1] Most Indian villages, with a population of 'less than 2,000 or around 400 families, cannot support a doctor'. More important, the families there are scattered and the villages do not have efficient transport or other infrastructure.

When a village has a population of more than 10,000, there are schools and recreational facilities. Therefore unlike the rest of India, during the early periods, there was no urban concentration of doctors in Kerala. They spread out everywhere, with the result that there was no shortage of medical manpower. The availability of medical manpower was crucial in the simple technological intervention of maternal and child care which led to better health indices.

Being a public health specialist, Anand is aware of the usual lead-time for people to accept and assimilate new technologies. In his experience, he found that due to the impact of education, the lead-time is shorter in Kerala.

When a service is provided, they immediately utilize it, or when they read it in the newspaper that other villages have this facility, they also demand it.

Anand concluded that the right perception of needs in terms of priority and right type of vocalization of needs, initially contributed to a great extent to the better health care system in Kerala.

Menon subscribed to the view that the development process in Kerala was in response to the articulation of people's demands. He calls 'our social development model, a demand model and not a provider-based model'. At the same time he warns about the consequence of continuing a demand model.

After some time, it will lead to some kind of an ideological crisis – because we expect everything. We won't be willing to make sacrifices in the larger interests of the society. Everyone is organized and he/she gives an ideological flavour to demands. (In Kerala) even a white-collar employee is a (member of the) proletariat. He or she believes (in it) genuinely.

Critical of the existing demands of Kerala society, Ram says that 'an average Keralite only shouts at somebody'. He finds that Keralites prefer white-collar jobs, but they will do 'anything abroad'. Reflecting on how Kerala society has lost a lot of its values, he asks 'why is it that people who are getting unemployment dole, don't do any work? They could do something productive for the society. But they won't'.

Kerala's social development outliers

Tribals

But those groups, which are unable to vocalize their demands, are outliers in the Kerala social development scenario. From his extensive experience in tribal areas, Kannan concludes that 'the tribals' voice is not heard in the democratic process of Kerala. 'They are a minority. They are only less than one per cent. Nobody wants them. Their votes don't have any value. Since they are not militant, no one listens to their faint voice'.

As a result, tribals in Kerala are a group marginalized from the main stream development process and they pay a heavy price for maldevelopment.

I have seen starvation among tribals. Even deaths due to starvation. It is quite natural during their lean period. While we were conducting a survey among the tribals of Kasargodu, we accidentally encountered a starvation death ... Let us not talk about it ... But there is no starvation death in government records.

Menon says it is possible.

In the tribal belt of Attappadi, there are people who starve. They may even die. It may even go unreported. Among tribals there is neither the concept of starvation nor the concept that the state should not allow starvation to take place. So we won't even know whether there is any starvation. They will not raise their voice and protest. So deaths due to starvation are possible.

He says it is a matter of interpretation whether the death was due to starvation or not. 'But there are lots of deaths due to prolonged, inadequate nutrition and low calorie intake. Prolonged malnutrition makes them more vulnerable'. Menon says that death due to starvation will not happen in a town in Kerala. 'If ration supply stops for a week, even the ministry will be at stake.² Death due to starvation is impossible in Kerala towns'.

By snatching away their resources, the development process in Kerala have de-skilled the tribals. Kannan cites the case of *Korgas,* who previously had the skill of making beautiful bamboo products. 'They only could produce such beautiful hand made products. They have beautiful long, tapering fingers, with which they made amazing bamboo products'. But the encroachments to their land and deforestation have taken away their resources and their raw materials, de-skilling them in that process. Thus:

If we take the parameters of a civilized society, a man should have some asset, for example, land; or he should have some productive aspect, which would provide him income to sustain himself and his family. Now these tribals have none of these. It was not like this before. I mean, even ten years back, it wasn't like this.

The extent of marginalizing tribals stretches even to snatching away by urban folk, of those projects specifically meant for the tribals. Kannan cites the example of the multi-million anti-poverty scheme of afforestation where the original objective was to plant bamboos and reeds on the riverbanks. 'Instead of rebuilding the resource base of the tribals, which we had damaged, we diverted that money for planting acacia on the roadsides. We did not implement an anti-poverty scheme'.

Menon believes that the exploitation of the tribal folk in Kerala was mainly due to a wrong development strategy on 'our part'.

We had a misconception that 'access' is an important aspect of development and that infrastructure is development. So we tried to build up access everywhere. We still believe that roads are development. It is OK in other places, but not in tribal areas. Previously it was impossible for us to reach there. But when we built roads, it became just like our land. So we went and exploited them. They lost whatever they had – their land, resources and raw materials. But, if we had taken steps to understand the value of their land and culture, this wouldn't have happened. Now it is too late.

Once roads were built, outsiders had access to the tribals, and exploitation became easy.[3] The exploitation ranged from snatching away their land, making them labourers on their own land, to sexually exploiting the tribal women. The encroachers were dealing with a culture in which the values and the mores, including those relating to sex were different. It was easy for them to exploit the 'naive' indigenous people who are not exposed to 'development'.

Menon says that there is a new form of exploitation, which has much more destructive potential than the earlier forms of crude exploitation. He cites Attappady, a prohibited[4] tribal area, an enclave, as an example.

> There, tribals are being used to transport liquor and they are also used as carriers in sandalwood smuggling to Tamil Nadu. Then of course, *ganja* cultivation. The tribal is being criminalized. Being a lawbreaker, he cannot ask for his rights. He cannot avail of an IRDP[5] loan. He has to live in hiding under the support of the exploiter. It is very difficult even for a well-meaning government official to help him, because he is a criminal. This means that they are isolated and their identity is lost. This has much more destructive potential than the earlier forms of crude exploitation ... Being a criminal, he cannot complain, and seek help or justice, even when he is being crudely exploited. Overall it is a frightening and depressing situation. It happens in Idukki too.

The callousness of bureaucracy has also contributed to the distress of tribals. During the early eighties, officials in Attappady distributed weak and old bulls to the tribals in the 'work bull scheme'. These bulls originally meant to be butchered were brought from the neighbouring states. Menon strongly believes that exploitation of tribals are 'all done by the bureaucracy or with the connivance of the bureaucracy'. He compares tribal belts like Attappady to 'the darkest parts of Bihar', a resource-rich, but socially backward state, controlled by feudal landlords. There is nobody to question. The tribals do not know how to demand. Nobody has tried to conscientize them. The development benefits meant for the tribals are being made use of by non-tribals who swarmed Attappady in the 70s.

'They are also poor, but far better off than the tribals are. Tribe is only a channel for benefit to flow to them'.

Kannan feels that we have failed in tribal welfare because we have a tendency to oversimplify the complex concept of development.

> When we talk about people below the poverty line, we see only the poverty line. On the other hand if we look deep into the Indian reality, we can find a lot of hidden lines. There is the power line. Most of the people below poverty line are below power line also. Then we have the 'pollution line' based on caste structure, where there is both a physical and psychological distance between the upper and the lower castes.

Fisherfolk

Despite that fact that Kerala has an effective system of human resources data maintenance, even basic data on fisherfolk is not available. *Kerala Fisheries - An Overview* (1992) gives the total number of fishermen as 216,710, 'fishermen' including men, women and children. In other words, they have classified the fisherfolk population to male, female and children, which makes it impossible to compute the sex ratio among fisherfolk. The only figure that could be arrived at, i.e., sex ratio among adults, gives a dismal picture. The sex ratio for the adult population is 951 against the overall Kerala figure of 1036. Further, children of all ages is more than 55% of the adult population (76,900 children among 139,810 adults), which exceeds the average for all of Kerala.

Bose, who had been working with and for the fisherfolk of Kerala, feels that they have not been integrated into the mainstream society. In all indices of physical qualities of life, the score of fisherfolk is much lower than that of the Kerala average. Their life expectancy is less, and infant mortality and birth rates high. Bose confirms that even data on physical qualities of their lives are not available. He describes the life of ordinary fishermen:

> The boys and the head of the family go fishing. They will go early in the morning, and then men will sleep or drink during the rest of the day and create problems. The same routine continues day after day. Nothing special. They are not participating in society and so miss out on the development process. They don't see anything. They only see the sea. The same sea, the

same darkness. Day in and day out, the deterioration of the resources, ... the same frustrations...

The frustrations of the menfolk and their drunken behaviour usually culminate in beating up the womenfolk. The condition of fisherwomen is appalling.

They have to take care of everything – look after the kids, do household chores, go and sell fish and by the time men come back, they should have the food ready and waiting, and their fishing implements have to be mended.

With a workload much higher than the rest of the Malayali women, they have more morbidity too. They get married at a very early age; again unlike her counterparts in the mainstream society. Bose says most of the girls from the fishing community in Malabar still get married before the age of eighteen 'and give birth immediately'.

Appu says that the environmental sanitation on the coastal areas is very poor. Since all the wells are polluted with faecal matter and infested with worms, there is no safe drinking water for fisherfolk. With very high density of population, the drinking water is polluted above all acceptable or prescribed safety limits. Children are the worst victims. They get diarrhoea easily.

Even after taking the medicines, they go back and drink the same water and come back after three days.

These children are not just the victims of poor environmental sanitation. Occupational requirements of their parents keep them away from schools.

Fishing in the sea is not one man's job. It is a family job. Even children below the age of 10 participate in economic activity. So, education, to them, is uneconomical and fishing, more remunerative ... Even if they go to school, soon they become dropouts.

At least in one instance, the demand for a school in the coastal area was not met due to the lobbying by powerful vested interests. Bose recalls an almost unbelievable incident, which happened in Parappanangadi, a densely populated coastal area in northern Kerala. The birth rate here is very high and some families even have 'ten to twelve children'. For lack of space at home, family members sleep on the seashore, by turn.

When a group of 'radical youth' demanded a school in Parappanangadi, the education minister, a senior leader of a communal political party who was elected from Parappanangadi, refused to permit it. Bose observes:

> If a school is established, children will learn. When children learn, it will result in infiltration of new values into the families. Modern values will affect the minister's vote banks. Hence, he refused to give his sanction.

Bose argues that it is not the absence of plans or schemes targeted for the fisherfolk that has blocked social development of fisherfolk. Apart from the defective planning and execution of policies and programmes, Kerala has not tried to integrate the fisherfolk into the mainstream society. Bose is angry and critical of the attitude of government and society at large.

> We want them to be fisherfolk, we want them to be scheduled castes and scheduled tribes forever. So we must colonize them. We must keep them aloof. We must keep them separate. Otherwise why the hell should we construct housing colonies exclusively for the fisherfolk? Why should we have schools exclusively for children of fisherfolk? This is the process of retaining a backward community in the backyards forever. Even today we have that social stigma, which is reflected in our development activities.

This brings us to back to the hidden lines, which Kannan had mentioned. Like the tribals, fisherfolk in Kerala area also below the poverty line, power line and pollution line.

Approaches to development

Top-down approach

All the officials who were interviewed are of the opinion that in Kerala the approach to development is typically top-down; in some cases, more as an exception rather than as a rule, the participatory approach has been adopted.

Top-down approach was rampant in tribal development. The attitude of the officials in tribal welfare was that of superiority, as Menon analyzes, a transaction that 'you don't know anything; we will teach you'. Consider, for instance, agriculture. Even in cultivation on slopes, where tribals had time-tested knowledge, passed through generations of research and development, the officials taught them 'superior methods'. The tribals were following multiple cropping, then perceived by development experts as primitive, but now accepted universally as extremely scientific from a sustainable perspective. It was scientific in the sense that it took care of the difference in maturation period, it gave capacity to withstand adverse weather conditions, and it took care of the different manure zones and ensured optimum utilization of land. The experts imposed monoculture on the tribals. Their native wisdom of traditional medicines, imbedded in their lifestyle was branded primitive and treated with scorn. Experts decided what they should do and how they should live their lives. Instead of the eco-friendly huts they lived in, the experts 'gave them tiled houses'. Nobody asked them what they wanted. The providers were sure they were teaching them a better lifestyle.

However, 'we cannot question the intentions of the early government officials. They were sincere. It is just that nobody had thought about these aspects'. He feels that at present there is a change in our perceptions. Now the transaction, 'at least on paper is "we will study what you are doing, and let us see"'.

Menon is right when he says that the participatory approach is a recent concept and that it is easy to criticize with hindsight. At the same time, the damage has already been done.

In fisheries development also, we ignored the native wisdom. The development officials refused even to think that the simple fisherfolk had knowledge of fishing, seasons, climate, landing centres and other aspects of living by and off the sea.

Kerala had to pay a heavy price for this approach. For example, in fisheries development, around 70 per cent of the departmental funds are being utilised for building up landing centres, harbours or peeling sheds. Bose points out that 'on evaluation, we can see that the majority of the programmes aimed at building up infrastructure facilities have gone as wasteful expenditure'. For example, a good percentage of the landing centres cannot be utilised. Bonafide fishermen have traditional landing centres. Instead of identifying the traditional landing centres and developing them, 'we go on building landing centres and harbours'.

> Say, an MLA[6] wants a landing centre to be built in his constituency or a harbour to be built in his place. For example, Kollam–Neendakara is said to be an ideal site for a harbour. We have a harbour there and we have spent a lot of money in the last four plan periods. At the same time, a member of Parliament wants another harbour just near Neendakara, at Thankassery. So there is a scheme for developing another harbour in Thankassery.

Bose says that while the developers think that more harbours will produce more fish from the sea, it is not true. 'We are building infrastructure, without understanding the resource base. We are building landing centres without taking into account the movement of the fish'. As a result of the top-down approach and political interference, we end up having dead harbours and dead landing centres.

The top-down approach in rural development schemes in several cases has not only failed to eradicate poverty, but has even resulted in the extinction of some indigenous species of animals. Kannan says the extinction of indigenous cattle in Kerala was the result of import of exotic varieties. Loans under IRDP and DRDA schemes are available only for the purchase of exotic varieties of cattle

> I had a friend who was a veterinary surgeon – Dr. Cherian. He was an assistant project officer in DRDA, like me. I used to tell him about the cow we had at home. Where can I get a cow like that? Later we realized that in the process of introducing new upgrade varieties, we lost all the vernacular ones. We don't have Vechoor cows. That cow had a lot of advantages. She was a domestic animal, a member of the family who survived on leftovers and did not require exotic treatment.

Kannan attributes this phenomenon to top-level planning and top-down approach. The cattle loan and subsidy scheme was conceived, introduced and implemented by animal husbandry specialists, who have an alien education, and were oriented more towards western technology and values.

We carry out indicative planning for every plan period. At the macro level we aim at increasing milk production. Then we will design micro level planning which involves decision to introduce high breed cattle. Then we decide that we should give two cows to a beneficiary.

Kannan argues that this 'is theoretically fine', but does not have any connection with grass-root realities or 'field compulsions'.

People who take up these loans are people with a lot of problems, people without much education. Moreover they have a lot of built-in constraints, constraints caused by their lives. It might be very difficult to look after these exotic cattle.

These exotic cattle need special feeds produced in the market. Their resistance to diseases being low, they need special medical attention and they need more living space, which is scarce in densely populated Kerala, more so, among the poor.

The introduction of a 'western model of development' has also affected women adversely.

Now men run everything. Getting a loan, meeting the village extension officer, searching for the cow, getting the approval from the vet. surgeon, all these are done by men. And the cattle give plenty of milk, which is sold by men and so the income goes to men. Virtually it is the men who benefit. But in the past, milk was for domestic consumption. Every house used to have a cow. Bringing up a cow was for household use, and money from selling the extra milk or yoghurt, butter or ghee, went to the female folk. In those days all the money generated from cattle, however small it may be, went to the females.

Thus women's traditional access to surplus proceeds has been cut off and generally speaking, men who now tend to monopolize the business also tend to squander money on liquor etc.

Participatory approach

The absence of a more participatory approach in development is the result of a combination of several factors including centralized planning, lack of awareness of grass root realities and a somewhat arrogant perception, usual in the top down approach to development, that the beneficiary is ignorant. There is another important factor, which is quite significant in the Kerala context:

> Community decisions ... poor people taking a decision or thinking together have been destroyed by our political processes. So you expect always to talk to leaders. I feel the failure in Kerala social development is either having lost it or haven't thought about it – always talk to the representatives and the representatives have limitations to represent.

Menon brought home a point on the organized social behaviour in Kerala. In Kerala everybody is unionized and organized. The same individual has both communal and political identities. This phenomenon while helping collective bargaining, hold back development processes to a great extent. As Menon remarks, it is good in conflict situations, but not when decisions have to be taken collectively on developmental activities. 'When we ask where the road should be, it is absurd to say "go and ask our leaders"'.

Apart from the tendency of people to leave decision-making to their leaders, the officials also find it easy and convenient to talk to representatives. At times this resulted in a nexus of bureaucracy, politicians and contractors. In a democratic set up there has to be political participation, intervention and involvement in development activities. But at the same time, it could also lead to undue political interference as pointed out by most of the officials interviewed. But Kannan had a different view.

> The complaints about political interference are correct and at the same time wrong. There is lot of temptation for the political activists. As the number of political activists increase and the scope and dimensions increase and when demand is more than supply and as long as there are officials willing to comply even with their unjust demands, there will be interference.

By citing his experience with implementation of a housing scheme for the oppressed classes, Kannan explained his case in point that if the officials are objective and impartial there won't be interference and that quality of services can be improved.

I returned to block development work after a long span of deskwork in the secretariat. When I went back to the field, housing schemes were being implemented with the vigour of a social movement. Houses were being built for low-income groups from scheduled castes and scheduled tribes under the *Indira Avaz Yojana*. Hundreds of houses were being built. I forgot the exact number. I asked: What is the criterion for allotment? Then my colleagues told me that there is a committee consisting of Block Development Officer, official from Scheduled Caste Development Department, Panchayat President and MLA. The Panchayat President will give a list, MLA will give another and on the basis of this list, what could be called a 'compromise list' will be evolved. Since the MLA might belong to one party and the Panchayat president to another, there will be tough competition. Then we get additional lists from the ministers. The practice was that a final list was made from all these lists. When I enquired, I found that almost all possible beneficiaries listed are deserving. Since the supply is less than demand, most of them pay bribes – even by borrowing.

What should be the objective criterion? I asked around. Nobody had a way out. At that time Menon was the collector.[7] He said, let us try to evolve a criterion. We decided, ladies first. You should remember that in *harijan*[8] colonies, there are quite a few deserted women, women who have been deserted after they had a couple of children. They will get the first priority. After exhausting their list, the next category – widows. Then physically disabled women. Then, physically disabled men. Later we will take the MLA's and Panchayat President's list. It won't be necessary, because by then the allotment will be exhausted.

When the committee assembled, there were members with lists in their pockets. Since I had to brief the committee in the beginning, I said, we need a criterion for allotment and I explained the suggested criterion and assured them that all these categories of people are below poverty line. The committee members agreed. In Kerala, nobody speaks out in the open against justice and fairness. Thus during that particular year people without any recommendation got houses allotted. People who never expected to get allotment. Only the first and second categories – the deserted women and widows were allotted houses. There wasn't any scope for the next category. Next year, for the same scheme, we asked the people of the colony to select the beneficiaries on the suggested criterion. They sat around, discussed and selected the beneficiaries.

It is true that if the objectives are objective and impartial, participatory approach is possible in Kerala. Menon shared his experience of popular participation in another housing project at Thankassery. Around one hundred and fifty houses were destroyed by fire in the coastal area of Thankassery. When the authorities decided to build houses for the poor fisherfolk, they attempted the approach of popular participation.

> I thought let us go beyond the formal consultative process – some kind of participatory approach. We held a meeting in the collector's conference hall.[9] Then I realized the potential of people's participation. All the hundred fifty five families were present. The very fact that they were sincerely consulted, that their identity was being recognized and that they have been talked to and that response was expected...even if we succeeded in giving that feeling, half the job is done. At that time it was not a symbolic action. Only later I realized the symbolic significance.

Menon recalls that the approach yielded results. A series of decisions which would have been very difficult, or even impossible to take in the normal bureaucratic top down approach were taken amicably. People raised ethical questions.

> Then there was an objection. Among those people who lost houses were people who already had sold the houses provided by the government and settled on seashores. Some of the participants in the meeting argued that the government providing houses again to them was unethical.

Menon and his team of officials found that there were several practical issues involved in this ethical issue. The government cannot trace the old records to identify those people who already had availed of and misused the benefits. It was just impossible. But the issue was resolved during the process of discussion. It was decided that the participants would inform the names of those people to a sub-collector in confidence. A list would be published, giving the chance for people listed to challenge the list. Again, in the absence of perfect records of previous households and the exact location of their houses, allotment might have been very difficult. There again the meeting came to a consensus that the beneficiaries themselves would discuss and decide on the site of the houses and in the event of disagreement, allotment would be made on the basis of lots.

The housing scheme was implemented. The local community participated in all construction activities, they executed the project with the help of government and non-governmental agencies. This was made possible among the fishing community of Kerala. The conventional belief is that they are a very volatile kind of people. It is true that this specific area had always been an area of conflict, where clashes between the ordinary fisherfolk and motorized fishing lobby were quite common. This proves that participatory approach could be effective even among a highly volatile group and that their collective spirit could be utilized for constructive purposes, to their advantage.

Another housing scheme, this time among tribals, provides further evidence on the scope and potential of original and creative problem solving. Since the supply was much less than the demand, the question of deciding who were to be allocated houses had to be addressed. Everybody in that tribal community deserved better housing.

> Then a young tribal came out with a suggestion. 'Let the old be allotted houses'. Everybody laughed at him. He said, 'No. I've a reason. A house is a dream for everyone. If the old people don't get houses now, they won't ever get it. Others have more time to hope for and look forward. So it is only ethical that the elderly be given houses first'.

Menon says that everyone assembled agreed immediately. Then there was only one serious problem. There are lots of elderly people in the community. How to identify the oldest people?

> They don't have birth certificates and all that. They don't even have the concept of numbers. But they all discussed and finally came to a conclusion. They all knew who is elder than whom. Being a very close knit community, they even know by how many days or even hours one person is elder or younger to another.

By community participation, community decisions were arrived at and the housing scheme was implemented successfully.

Ramu believes that it is possible to implement development schemes with popular participation, despite the resistance from vested interests at every stage. 'But the initiative has to come from the officials'. He observes that even schemes, which are to be implemented with public participation, are now being done by contractors. He cites the construction of a road in Pathanapuram Taluk, a road that was named as 'people's road'.

> In 1989–90, there was a scheme for construction of a road in Pathanapuram Taluk under the Rural Landless Employment Generation Scheme. Theoretically all work coming under the scheme should be executed by a people's committee. But it never happened. On the records there were people and committee. But in reality, it would be the contractors and engineers. The estimate would be prepared by government engineers. They knew how to make a profitable estimate and no one would get head or tail of it. There will be some m³ and all that. A contractor was be the head of the non-existent committee, who made a profit and a share of which went to the officials and politicians.

When a group of district officials wanted to form a genuine beneficiary committee, it was met with resistance. The minister, popular for pro-poor attitudes and who had launched effective public distribution schemes represented the constituency. He called in the senior official and told him that 'this is all utopian' and asked him whether he was trying to jeopardize development work in his constituency,

Ramu says the officials went forward, formulated people's committee and explained the work. Translating the estimate to people's language – so many baskets of sand, so many baskets of rubble and so on, they demystified the estimate and posted these statistics on the sites. The officials made the whole process transparent.

After overcoming the resistance from the public works department-contractor-politician lobby, the road was constructed at 40 per cent of the estimated cost and with the balance amount, they extended the road even further.

Ramu recalls that the whole construction activity was like a festival. He says that it is possible to involve people if Kerala bureaucracy abandons its impersonal attitudes, and does its job 'with more personal involvement and personal touch'.

There are several instances of the popular participatory approach being used successfully in Kerala, the literacy mission in the early 1990s, the resource mapping programme and the aftermath of the programme, especially in Kallassery, all of which point towards a new direction in participatory development processes.

Women in Development

Nair says that despite high literacy and education of women in Kerala, they have very limited role in decision making at the social level, which poses a major challenge for development efforts, especially in the water and sanitation sector. 'While women are responsible for water and sanitation around the home, they have a weak voice in negotiations and decisions about many aspects important for themselves and their children'. Even women who are engaged in income generating activities, and who do all household work including fetching water, collecting fuel, washing clothes and taking care of children and elderly still do not come out and explain their opinions openly. From his vast experience, Nair found that rural women, adhering to cultural norms, are 'generally shy to express themselves in mixed meetings. They are not always taken seriously when they do speak'.

Changes are taking place, though slowly. Women are now consulted in sanitation programmes. Since women are the prime users of public taps, they are consulted on the location of such installations; which in turn ensures 'public commitment to the care and use of the water taps'.

Poor women, previously working as unskilled construction labourers, mainly mixing concrete and carrying loads are now given training in construction activities by the socio-economic units of the Kerala Water Authority. To ensure equality, they are given the same wages as male masons, a practice still unheard of in the traditional construction sector of Kerala.

In rural development, there are specific schemes for women. IRDP has a component solely for the development of women and children in rural areas. Under this scheme, assistance is given to a group of ten or fifteen women for making garments, pillows, pickles etc. – that could be done at home. Kannan has found that women's collective schemes are successful because:

> Women here psychologically stick together. For example, if we look at rural bus stops, women waiting for the bus stick together. Men don't. They stand alone.

Further, the family benefits more when women earn.

If I were to make a rule-of-thumb assessment, I would say that the income generated from these schemes goes to the family and to recycle the existing units. Men are not really that careful in spending money.

Though women's earnings find their way home more than that of men, men prefer not to involve women in group activities. Appu says that a women's development programme launched in Malappuram is called the 'community based nutritional programme'. 'Even though there is no nutrition, we call it like that because otherwise men would never allow women to come out'.

He says that Malappuram is the first district in India where family group networks of women have been set up for self-help. 'Women who have never stepped out of their homes are now coming out to take up NABARD (National Agricultural Bank for Rural Development) loans and to start ventures'.

This scheme which Appu hopes would make 'a tremendous impact within five years from now' is a collective of women, who got together, pooled their resources, charted out schemes and are implementing them. They provide loans to members of the group and 'there is no external interference'. The government machinery is extending full co-operation. The membership at the time of the interview was 42,000.

The total savings of these 42,000 women come to 3 million. NABARD is willing to give another 9 million. The total amount comes to 12 million.

Bose described how a small scheme for women's development could be effective for a short while and be transformed to a larger scheme and made ineffective. During 1988–89, the fisheries department started a very simple scheme – giving small loans to the fisherwomen for buying fish vending implements. Till then fisherwomen used to carry their load of fish in bamboo baskets lined with plastic sheets. It was difficult and inconvenient in the sense that the water would seep through the baskets on to their faces and bodies. With the implementation of this scheme, they all switched over to aluminium vessels covered with rubber sheets, which are leak proof even though the fish are covered with ice.

All the banks came forward. There were three loan schemes of Rs. 500, 600 and 750 @ 7 per cent interest. They need repay only after six months. If they can repay before that, fine, they get another loan. They can use the money to buy fish and implements.

The scheme was running successfully till there was a change in the ministry.

The new ministry thought this scheme was started by the earlier ministry. Why should we promote it and give them the credit?

In Kerala, there are no full stops. Schemes take new forms and new labels. Since the earlier ministry had a fisheries bank in the pipeline, the new ministry came out with the concept of a women's bank. In reality, there is a niche for a women's bank that would give them small loans, in all walks of society, especially for fisher women. At present these women depend on loan sharks. 'When they borrow Rupees 100 today morning, they get Rupees 90 in hand and they have to return Rupees 100, the next day'.

However, the implementation of the scheme leaves much to be desired. There are instances of men taking up these loans and then lending the money at exorbitant rates of interest. 'Since there is no check measure the scheme cannot be implemented effectively'.

Additionally, the women's bank gives big loans, for purchasing autocarriers and lorries for transporting fish. Loans involving huge sums are given to groups. Bose says that when the money involved was small, there was not much of a problem; but when the scale expanded, new problems have cropped in.

Problems in the formation of groups – political groups, communal groups ... Congress vehicles, Communist vehicles, Kerala Congress[10] vehicles, and so on and so forth.

Now there are intermediaries 'arranging loans' and intra-group conflicts. Since only some members of the group would be keen on repaying, there is conflict among members as to the ownership of the vehicles. 'While theoretically, it (the scheme) is for the welfare of women, in practice, men utilise and misuse the scheme'.

Liberalization in Kerala[11]

Liberalization, in a broad sense, refers to the process of the reduction in the role of the state and an increase in the role of the market. Economic deregulation and privatization of state owned enterprises and integration into the world economy through foreign investment are the key strategies of liberalization. Liberalization also implies a reduction of government's distributive function which often entails reducing or eliminating subsidies to producers and consumers (Tschirgi, 1996). The government of India started its new economic policy of liberalization in 1991, as a result of the World Bank/IMF Structural Adjustment Programme (Shiva, 1996).

All the officials interviewed, except two, felt that the liberalization process has had very little impact on Kerala so far. In the health sector, the government has started encouraging local initiatives and is now willing to collaborate with the private sector. For fear of criticism, these efforts have not been given much publicity.

To give an example, in Perunthalmanna government taluk hospital, a blood bank has been started with government-private collaboration. The government gave permission to private hospitals and the IMA (Indian Medical Association) of Perunthalmanna to construct a building for a blood bank on Taluk hospital premises. The equipment was supplied by the government under the AIDS prevention programme.

> The staff is appointed by the managing committee, consisting of four private hospital representatives and four IMA members and they run it and the government granted permission to open a separate bank account. They charge fees at concessionary rates to the Taluk hospital patients. Because it is done jointly, private hospitals have not set up their own private blood banks. Whenever they require blood, they rush to the Blood Bank. They also have an interest in seeing that it runs well because it saves a lot of investment and maintenance. To keep the high quality is in their interest too. Spic and spac. Highly clean and sterilized. Everybody is wearing uniforms and gloves.

There has also been a change in the attitude of the government towards the health sector. Appu says that the concept of the charity hospital (*Dharmasupathri*) is gone.

> We can give 40 to 50 per cent of people free treatment. But we cannot give free treatment to 100 per cent patients in government hospitals.

By introducing outpatient (OP) ticket charges in the government hospitals, Appu feels that some amount of money is generated which can be used for improvement and maintenance of hospital facilities and equipment.

> The system of writing notes to the DMO (District Medical Officer) for purchase of even a small (light) bulb has to stop.

Appu feels that the liberalization efforts have resulted in correcting wrong priorities practised for a long time. Public health is an area in which the private sector is reluctant to get involved. He thinks that primary health care for preventive aspects, cure of infectious diseases and nutritional aspects are the government's responsibility. Since the private sector 'will not take care of it', the government should really put money in'. As a part of reorientation of priorities, the government is correcting the distortions that have already taken place in the health care expenditure pattern. But unfortunately the politicians persistently demand more money for Medical Colleges.

> Everybody is talking about why money is not coming to medical colleges. When I have subject committee meetings with MLAs, 95 per cent of the discussions is on inadequacies of the Medical Colleges. Nobody speaks for primary health. In Kerala, everybody who is somebody goes to Medical College for treatment. See the minutes of the meetings. Nobody speaks about primary health centres.

Despite the pressure, the government is now channelling money to the rural health centres rather than to Medical Colleges. The liberalization attempts have also resulted in cutting down expenditure on food in government hospitals. Appu justifies the action:

> We found that expenditure on food can marginally be reduced because people admitted in hospitals are anyway bringing food from their homes. The bulk of the food items, which we were supplying to the hospital, is actually getting diverted to the black market.

He says that the government policy now is that food will be given only where the doctor prescribes a special diet for the patients. Instead of providing food universally, it is now restricted to poor people. Since the food and medicine are combined under one account heading in the budgetary provision, the savings from food expenditure is used for buying medicines.

> The government is in the process of introducing an effective self financing system and giving autonomy to the hospital development committees. Since 'people in Kerala feel that if it is government, it has to be free', it is the hospital development committee which charges and collects money for hospital services. Besides OP ticket charges, the government has also introduced the system of charging for various services and medicines 'from people who can afford it'. Unlike the usual government system of remittance, the money collected from patients is kept in the respective hospitals. The hospital development committee can utilise the money for buying medicines for the poor, repair and maintenance of hospital equipment. To that extent flexibility has been given to the people in the field'.

Another area in which liberalization has made an impact is on health education. New courses are started even in Taluk Headquarters hospitals. At Kodungallur, the hospital development authority has started home nursing courses. Out of thousands of applicants, they selected thirty girls to be trained in home nursing. This also provides nursing support in the government hospital.

Since 1995, stipends for nursing students have been discontinued. The government feels that while providing stipends was essential at the initial stage to attract people to the nursing profession, it is no longer necessary. The government also plans to increase tuition fees for medical education.

> The aim is that if you are getting a job once you complete the course, why should government subsidize the entire amount? We are reasonably phasing out the subsidy. We revised the MBBS fees from Rupees 350 to Rupees 1,600 ... We hope to slowly step up the amount so that at least a share of the amount will be borne by the student. Right now the subsidy per medical student is Rupees 150,000 a year.

To the question as to how poor people can afford to send their children for medical education, Appu replied that there could be scholarships and soft loans. He estimates that around 200 to 500 million rupees goes out of the state to finance medical education alone. He says that while Kerala has two dental colleges, Bangalore, the capital of the neighbouring state Karnataka, has twenty two dental colleges and 50 per cent of the students there are from Kerala. In 1994, Tamil Nadu government set up 375 colleges – for nursing, laboratory technology, pharmacy etc. and it is estimated that at least 25 per cent of the students in these colleges are from Kerala.

> Like any other industry where market forces do intervene, why not in medical education in Kerala? This will result in regional economic development too.

If the change in ministry does not result in a change of plans, Kerala will have a few medical-education institutions in the private sector. Appu says that 1,300 Malayali doctors in the United States are willing to invest US $15,000 each to start a medical college in Kerala. With this capital of US $ 19.5 million dollars, the health official hopes that a medical college could be set up. He says, one of the conditions of the US doctors 'may be that a place be given to their kid'. Both the state and the non-resident Indians (NRIs) would benefit from this collaboration. For the NRIs, it is much more economical to send their children to Kerala and as for the state, which is facing fiscal crisis, investment is ensured.

> The advantage is that they want the institution in which these kids study to be very good. They'll ensure that. Assuming that fifty of them (the NRI doctors) can take one year's leave by rotation and come as visiting professor, we will have a good strength of staff. We will have a top class educational institution. Why should we say no?

Bose explained how liberalization is adversely affecting the poor fisherfolk of Kerala.

Liberalization policies of the central government have resulted in issuance of deep sea fishing licences to multi national companies. This has affected traditional fisherfolk adversely. Since there is depletion of resources, they are also compelled to venture into deep sea fishing, for which they need mechanized vessels. They are availing themselves of loans of up to three million rupees to purchase an OBM (out board motor engine), the market for which is monopolized by Japanese firms. Fishing in deep sea using OBM engines, require factory made nets. The new dependence on factory made nets has displaced women making and mending nets. The mechanization has also resulted in additional costs. The fisherfolk have to invest in fuel, with the result that the price of fish in Kerala has gone sky high. The fishermen who are illiterates or semi-literates are handling the sophisticated OBM engines, with the result that the engines get damaged quite fast. The dependency starts from availing huge loans and extends to servicing and maintenance of the engines.

With the arrival of the Multi-National Corporations (MNCs), a lot of ice factories engaged in freezing fish had no option, but to wind up their operation, because MNCs started sophisticated plants enabling IQF (individually quick frozen) processing. This also displaced a lot of women workers or degraded them to contract labourers.

Bose warns of the eco-disaster in store for Kerala by introducing aquaculture with participation of MNCs. He recalls what has happened in Nelloor of Andhra Pradesh, where all the paddy fields and wells were polluted due to aquaculture.[12] Bose says that the liberalization policies of the government in fisheries sector will result not only in over-dependency on capital and technology, but also in eco-abuse.

Future

The responses of the officials on the future of Kerala society, the role of government and social development process in Kerala are rather mixed. While all those interviewed agreed that development in Kerala had reached a cross-roads, some were sceptical and others were optimistic about the prospects and directions for future developments. Irrespective of the differences in perceptions of the future, most of them think that several services, which are now universally free, have to be limited to the poor and the needy. They are also aware of the difficulties in limiting the subsidies on the basis of means testing, for, as Menon puts it, 'only the government officials have proper income records'.

Hoping that he is wrong, Appu says:

> Kerala can very well go back to a very bad situation if we are not careful, because our alcoholism is very high. People are becoming alcoholic at an early age. In the last decade the age has dropped by more than ten years.

People are becoming alcoholics in their late twenties, rather than as (previously) in their early forties.

He is of the opinion that Keralites are 'very shallowly looking at some indicators. Nobody is bothered about morbidity. Life expectancy is high. We are keeping everybody alive. But how well are we keeping them alive?' He estimates that Keralites are consuming medicines worth 1.5 billion rupees every year, much higher than the consumption of medicines worth 1.2 billion rupees in Tamil Nadu, a state having a much higher population.[13] 'I am worried about what will happen twenty years from now. We will have a population, which is highly over-drugged, and drug resistant.'

He criticized 'our tendency to pat ourselves too much on our back, saying we are number one, without realizing that we can't remain number one easily, it can be done only by a continuous process of improvement. This is not taking place. Public health education has fallen quite dramatically, though people have become health conscious'.

Kannan is optimistic on the future of development in Kerala. He agrees that the money, the state can invest in social sectors is limited, and is getting reduced due to the fiscal crisis. The expenditure can be planned more optimally and efficiently, so that better service can be provided with lower expenditure, thus improving the quality of service. On the basis of his experience with rural Kerala, Kannan feels that wherever the government is withdrawing, 'people are rushing in'. This is visible especially in the education sector. The present initiatives of public participation and the emergence of Panchayati Raj system 'are expected to trigger off a process of true decentralization and micro-level planning which would consolidate Kerala's achievement in the field of social development'.

The present indicators show the possibility of evolving a model that would satisfy people's development needs, without investing more and with the same expenditure pattern. Right now these efforts are scattered. At the same time, Kerala society is preparing for a leap towards a new Kerala model.

Anand is of the opinion that unless there is a change in attitudes in Kerala society, there is no hope. As for the bureaucracy, 'we go by the rotten rules and queries, disbelieving everybody. We have perfected institutional inefficiency, not even as an art, but as a science'. He thinks the vocalization of demands in Kerala is a story of the past. 'Now people have become philosophically reconciled to incompetence. We have become a paralyzed, numb society'. He feels that only when there is a change in the attitude of bureaucracy and the public, can Kerala go forward. Kannan also expressed the same view saying that the 'huge, slow and cynical government bureaucracy', 'without any openness in functioning' stands in the way of social development in Kerala.

With an optimistic note on the future of Kerala development, Arjun says that the state is paving the way for increased participation of private entrepreneurs and groups. The social development efforts are becoming more focused and need based through participation of large voluntary organizations and non-governmental organizations and through decentralized decision making mechanisms. These efforts, he hopes, will yield results. He believes that social development will result in economic development.

> The thrust of social welfare activities is to develop a social infrastructure accommodating the entire spectrum of the population. By developing a good infrastructure the objective is to provide an environment which is conducive for economic activities to sprout and prosper. Once this is triggered, the per capita income levels would get boosted.

Menon argues that the major factor not conducive to growth, was that debureaucratization did not take place in Kerala and that provision of social services is dependent on a large government staff. He hopes that state intervention in Kerala will yield more results by focusing on the needy and targeting subsidies, ensuring greater efficiency in the service delivery mechanisms and facilitating investment by focusing on the human resource potential. With greater involvement of people and more planning at multiple levels with particular emphasis on the grass roots level planning, Kerala can improve its social development. Citing certain institutions in labour relations and welfare, unique to Kerala, like organized sectors for all occupational groups, industrial relations committees ensuring tri-party settlement and welfare funds with 'quite a huge sum of resources' Menon argues that working class will improve their lives in the future Kerala. 'With the money in welfare funds, they can invest in education and health sectors and can ensure certain percentage of beds for themselves and their families and a few places for their children in higher education institutions. The possibilities are immense'. He feels that organized worker's involvement in development pursuits will benefit society at large.

Conclusion

This chapter, organized on the basis of specific questions to the government officials, broadly reflects the development scene in Kerala. All the officials were self-critical and most of them were not satisfied with what Kerala has achieved. Their frankness and critical evaluation itself to a great extent reflects the value Keralites ascribe to freedom of expression. Several senior bureaucrats in Kerala are writers and columnists, most often, critical of bureaucracy and society at large. This has a tremendous impact on Kerala society, where media is treated with respect. One major aspect of Kerala society is the freedom of expression of people at large. In Kerala, big brother is not watching.

Most of the officials agreed on the genesis of the development path in Kerala. A combination of the efforts of benevolent rulers (especially of Travancore), introduction of westernization processes (by the Christian missionaries) and a people's movement (mostly led by communist parties) have contributed to social development in Kerala. These historical factors gave an impetus for the state government to pursue social development goals. At the same time, as pointed out by Kannan and Menon, ad-hocism in planning has adversely affected the development process in Kerala. Since Kerala had been following a 'demand model' (Menon), the development pursuits have excluded minority groups like tribals and fisherfolk, who were unable to vocalize their demands.

While the planning process was in response to people's demands, the implementation of policies and programmes lacks people's participation, further marginalizing the minority groups. On the one hand, bureaucracy in Kerala followed a top-down approach and on the other hand, people delegated the authority to their representatives.

Most of the officials interviewed admitted that the Kerala development process generally ignored women, but wherever women have been involved, the results of the schemes and projects were remarkable.

Neo-liberalism seems to have invaded the collective consciousness of Kerala bureaucracy. The withdrawal of the state from education and health sectors and the superiority ascribed to market mechanisms point to this direction. Most of the officials believed that liberalization has not made much impact on Kerala society. But interviews with the health and fisheries officials reveal that it is not so. The plight of the fisherfolk and the potential eco-degradation due to aquaculture and globalization are not yet on the general bureaucratic agenda. Since liberalization in 1991, the prices of essential commodities distributed through PDS have gone up steadily,[14] adversely affecting the poor people of Kerala, who already face severe unemployment.

In a sense, the crisis of a welfare state is reflected in most of the interviews. The state provisions seem to discourage self-reliance, standing in the way of individual provision and responsibility. Kerala is at a cross-roads, not sure of which path to take.

Having looked into the perceptions of development officials, let us see the grass-root realities and analyze the quality of life of people in three panchayats.

Notes

1   Peterson and Peterson (1986) have also made similar observation. 'One reason for the better educational, health, and family-planning facilities in Kerala has been that there most villages are settlements of more than 10,000, where the provision of services is less cumbersome and far cheaper' (pp. 419–20).

2   The political parties in opposition will make this an issue, and the protests and demonstrations could take any unexpected course. These may even result in a 'no confidence motion' and resignation of the ministry.

3   Suresh (1991; p. 17), quotes the *Irula* (a tribe) leader, 'Your roads did shorten the distance between our villages and your towns, making transport easier, but they also brought in thousands of settlers who have displaced us completely from our land. The forest, which once covered our land and supplied us food, fodder, medicine and shelter, has disappeared. Cheated out of our property and wealth, robbed of our culture and pride, we are today made to live lives stricken with poverty, ignorance, disease'.

4   Liquor is prohibited here.

5   Integrated Rural Development Programme.

6   Member of Legislative Assembly – usually an elected representative.

7   Chief of district administration.

8   Literally meaning God's children, for referring to scheduled castes; now no longer used in official communication.
9   Usually the Collectors' conference hall is meant for meetings with elites – politicians, community leaders and senior bureaucrats.
10   these are some of the leading political parties in Kerala.
11   So far, there has not been any serious study on the impact of liberalization in Kerala. For a discussion of the effects of liberalization at the national level, please refer Public Interest Research Group (1995) and Suryanarayana (1996).
12   Shiva (1996) has described the eco-disaster at Nelloor caused by aquaculture, in the 'Environmental Impact of Economic Globalization' (*Manorama Year Book*, 1996).
13   Tamil Nadu's population, as per 1991 census is 55.8 million against Kerala's 29.1 million.
14   For example, in 1990, the price of one kg. of rice was Rs. 3.28; by 1994, it became Rs. 6.84, by 1999, it became 9.40.

5 Grass-Roots Realities of Development

We have discussed the macro-level Kerala realities in the previous chapters. We shall now look deep into the grassroots realities of Kerala. From the micro-level data of three panchayats, we shall analyze the standard of living of people in these panchayats. These three panchayats, representing the geographical low, mid and high levels[1] of Kerala have been selected for understanding the living standards of people in all geographical divisions of Kerala. The data used for analysis is from the socio-economic data collected by the Centre for Earth Sciences (CESS) as part of a resource-mapping programme.[2] This programme, jointly undertaken by scientists, social scientists and panchayat officials, with the help of trained local level volunteers, is the first micro-level survey of geographical and socio-economic factors of Kerala. It was intended as a data bank for environmental and socio-economic appraisal of Kerala, and to help sustainable development planning at the grass-roots level (CESS, 1991).

The survey generated data on 3,389 households in the low-level panchayat, 3,503 households in the mid-level panchayat and 3,792 households in the high-level panchayat Thus altogether, data was generated for 10,684 households. CESS had entered raw data in dBASE IV. The coded data were entered in separate files. The first file on households had data on:

1. location (name of the panchayat, ward no. and survey no.);
2. Number of members;
3. social class and religion of the members;
4. Type of housing, tenure status, area of land on hand;
5. Cooking methods and fuel used;
6. Source and scarcity of drinking water;
7. Main source of income;

8. Employment of head of household and existence of household industry; and
9. Type of sanitation.

The second file on facilities and possessions had data on:

1. access to electricity; and
2. possession of following items:

    Radio, Television, Mixie, Refrigerator, Pressure cooker, Grinder, Washing machine, Cycle, Scooter/motor cycle, Car/jeep and Telephone.

In respect of the mid-level panchayat, an additional file was available with the following data on individual members of the family:

1. Sex;
2. Age;
3. Marital status and
4. Education.

Limitations of the data

The available data set had both advantages and disadvantages. That the data was collected for the population as a whole, is a major advantage. It would have been impossible for the researchers to conduct a survey, which would match the scale and magnitude of the resource mapping data.

One of the limitations of the sample is that it does not include a coastal or a tribal panchayat. Recent studies of the Kerala development experience treat both fisherfolk and tribals as 'outliers', implying that these sections of the society are still marginalized and have not yet benefited much from the development pursuits of Kerala society.[3] Another limitation is that three panchayats under study are situated in the southern part of Kerala. Hence the north-south disparities in development, if any, could not be analyzed.

The survey does not provide data on the health status of people, making it impossible to analyze the morbidity pattern in Kerala. Data on earnings are also not available. This is not a major limitation because, the data provide information on possessions and facilities. Though CESS had collected consumption pattern of households on essential commodities like rice, fish and vegetables, they were not made available to us. Again, though data on type of housing are collected in detail, data on the area (in sq. ft.) of houses are lacking. Nevertheless, the available data are capable of providing a good indication of the lifestyle of people in the three geographical divisions – low, mid and high lands of Kerala.

Processing the data

All the three panchayats have ten wards each. CESS had entered the data for the households; and the data for facilities and possessions for each ward under separate files. On going through the data, it was found that the quality of housing and sanitation in some wards was worse than in others. It also became clear that it was possible that poor people were more concentrated in some wards more than others. During visits to the panchayats it was confirmed that wards nearer to junctions and main roads had more middle-class and rich people, while wards further away form the main roads and junctions had a greater proportion of poor people. This prevented the adoption of any sampling method, for fear of losing the true picture. Hence the entire data set is used in the analysis.

The first step in data compilation was to bring together the data for all the 10 wards for the categories 'households' and 'facilities and possessions'. The next step was to combine these separate files into one master file for each panchayat. When the 'households' and 'facilities and possessions' files were combined, it resulted in a few entries being truncated. This happened because some entries were missing in either of the files. In the case of personal data analysis in the mid-level panchayat, compilation had to be extended to another level to include the data on individuals, bringing the total number of entries to 16,865[4] spread over 37 columns.

From the raw data, relevant information in tabular form was arrived at, by 'querying' the combined dBASE files.

Organization of the chapter

This chapter is organized into three sections – Section one consists of an overview of the panchayats, analysis of the demographic characteristics, habitation, sanitation, source and scarcity of drinking water and availability of facilities and possessions.

In Section two, by formulating an index of the level of poverty and affluence, the population is classified into very poor, poor, middle-class and rich. Chi square tests of significance[5] were conducted to assess the relationship between the following variables:

1.   Level of poverty and main source of income of households;
2.   Level of poverty and housing conditions;
3.   Level of poverty and sanitation;
4.   Level of poverty and social stratification;
5.   Level of poverty and source of drinking water;
6.   Level of poverty and type of cooking fuel;
7.   Level of poverty and type of cooking stove;
8.   Level of poverty and possession of consumer durables and
9.   Level of poverty and possession of land.

The Chi square tests of significance for the above variables were conducted for all the three panchayats under study. The inter-regional variations in the level of poverty/affluence and the living standards of the previously oppressed classes in relation to the general population are also assessed in this section.

In Section three, the educational and marital aspects of the household members of the mid-level panchayat are analyzed. Chi square tests of independence and coefficient of variation tests were conducted in order to understand the relationship between the various categories of sanitation and factors, which influence the type of sanitation.

Section One: Overview of the panchayats

Krishnapuram, the low-level panchayat

Kayamkulam, the town nearest to the low-level panchayat can be reached by bus or train. Travelling around three kms by bus or autorikshaw, we reach Krishnapuram junction. In the junction we see a small private hospital, a lower-primary school, few groceries, vegetable and panshops and a restaurant-cum-beer parlour run by the Kerala Tourist Development

Corporation. At all times of the day, the restaurant is filled with long-distance travellers and tourists; and the beer parlour with local men of all ages. Being summer, the well in the premises of the lower primary school is dry. The school toilet, intended for the exclusive use of teachers and other staff members, is locked. There is a strong stench from the compound wall. Near the junction is a temporary stall with the banner 'tender coconuts' – but they are selling soft drinks; and not tender coconuts!

We go into the panchayat, crossing the rails, confirming that the trains are not approaching. The low-level panchayat looks serene, with lots of fruit trees like mangoes and jack fruits. We see coconut trees everywhere. Even a government coconut research centre is situated in the low-level panchayat. The activity level is very low. Nothing seems to be happening, except for the busy laying of telephone cables by workers from Tamil Nadu.[6] They are contract labourers, wearing coloured dhothis and working very hard under the scorching sun. The Malayali contractor has imported twenty workers from Tamil Nadu. They have rented a small house, where they cook and eat. Once the work is finished, they go back to their village in Tamil Nadu, with their small savings, which they said, would go a long way in their village.

Walking through the interiors of the panchayat, we see occasional lorries, carrying construction materials, autorikshaw taxis, filled with more than it's carrying capacity, passing cyclists and people waiting patiently for the bus to the town. Thatched tea shops have few customers, most of them reading sheets from the morning newspapers, even in the afternoon. We see palatial concrete buildings, next to thatched huts. The sanitation facilities of the poor are dismal. Water in the wells looks greyish white. Pit toilets, with walls made of palm leaves or coloured cloth stand very close to the wells. Most of the toilets are broken and excreta seeps into the nearby canals.

In this landscape of poverty, we meet an elderly pan-shop owner, looking much older than his 65 years of age. His story reflects the dilemmas faced by the people of Kerala society in education. Ramakrishnan Nair has two daughters – the eldest with a post-graduate degree in Botany, and the youngest, with an undergraduate degree in Economics, both of whom are unemployed. They had been trying for jobs, ever since they finished high school. Nair says, he has sold whatever land he had, which was not much anyway, to educate his daughters, and he has only five cents of land (5% of an acre), with the hut on it. He had hoped that education would provide his daughters with a passport for a better life. Now all he wants is to see them married off. But, since his daughters are university educated, prospective bridegrooms without university degrees will not be prepared to marry them. Despite the fact that they are educated, he cannot marry them off, without paying dowry. He says, he does not have any money left. He is a diabetic patient and has to go every day to the nearest public health centre to get injections. 'No. The health centre will not supply medicines. They do not have any medicines. So I buy medicine from the medical shop every day and wait in the queue to be injected. I do not know what is in store for my daughters or for me'.

In the lower-primary school in the panchayat, the teachers complain about the scarcity of water, the scarcity of resources, and how 'anti-social elements' throw rubbish into the school well. The teachers say that despite all the constraints, the school has been able to cater to the children from poor families. They find the noon-meal programme very effective. All the children, irrespective of their family income, share the afternoon meals. 'When the supply of rice and dal is delayed, we bring it from our homes. How can we do nothing seeing the tired faces of the small kids?' a senior teacher asked. Even amidst the lack of affluence, people in the low-level panchayat are willing to share whatever they have, even with a stranger like me. In the One Lakh Housing Colony, we see only poverty around. No proper drinking water, no sanitation, no electricity and even the street lights do not have bulbs. Despite poverty and lack of basic amenities, all boys and girls in the colony attend schools, and parents pin their hopes on these children.

The rich in the panchayat, like anywhere else in Kerala have horrible flat-roofed concrete houses, with garishly painted walls, and mosaic-tiled floors. Antennas protrude from the terrace. The strong compound walls keep away intruders and even a moment's pause in front of the iron gate provokes the dogs inside to bark non-stop.

An elderly widow lives alone in a single room hut, in the neighbourhood of the neo-rich. She cannot remember her age; she might be in her late seventies or early eighties. The broken frame of her thick eye glasses is tied up with a faded black string. She says she cannot see properly. Her son has set up a nuclear family in another panchayat. She has a well and takes a bath at its edge. Her hut has electricity; and a 15 V bulb is hanging from the bamboo roof. For the past three months she has not received the widow's pension. Having no toilet facility is a 'very serious problem', because once the sun sets, she cannot see anything and she occasionally falls down when she goes to the nearby open space to attend nature's calls. 'Can you help me?' she asks.

Andoorkonam, the mid-level panchayat

The first impression on reaching the mid-level panchayat of Andoorkonam is that it has more urban features than the low-level and the high-level panchayats. The mid-level panchayat is more like a town. The junction has a big co-operative bank, a Maveli store, a mini-bus-station and rows of concrete buildings on both sides of the road. The mid-level panchayat has quite a few shops at the junction; selling textiles, groceries, fruits and vegetables, medicine, sanitary wares, etc. People go in and out of the STD/ISD telephone booth, where the owner-cum-manager of the establishment said, the entire telephone network of the mid-level panchayat was dead for the last two days and that the lines started functioning just then.

We see around twenty autorikshaws waiting for prospective clients. The junction is buzzing with activity. As we go forward, we see a garishly painted concrete building with a huge dish antenna installed on the terrace. In the tiny room on the ground floor is a video cassette-lending library, with a huge advertisement on the glass panel – 'fax facility available'. Going forward, we see a shop stacked with stoves made of baked clay. An Ambassador car, sounding its horn madly, is overtaking a bullock cart fully loaded with coconut husks. Before the unmanned level-crossing, we see a grocery-cum pan shop. The 14-inch portable black and white television faces the owner of the shop, a man in his early thirties, a Gulf-returnee. The Sony tape recorder is playing popular Malayalam film songs. Walking past the telephone exchange building, we see three women breaking rocks into rubble, with a hammer, beneath a banyan tree. Two children, wearing coloured dhothis and blue and pink shirts are playing and helping these women simultaneously. They are Vasumathi's children, both studying in the nearby high school. Being summer vacation, she wants to avoid her children hanging around, so there they are, helping their mother. She gets three and a half rupees for breaking a basket of stones. She is a coir-worker, working in the nearby co-operative and in the evenings and on Sundays, she breaks stones for the contractors. She has studied up to standard VIII and says she wants her children to study well, go to college, and get a degree. 'Otherwise how will they survive?' She has a small hut on two cents of land, about ten minutes walk from the junction. No, she does not have electricity. She does not have a toilet. 'Men can manage somehow or the other. For us women, we can attend the call of nature only during late evenings or early mornings, even before sunrise'. She finds it difficult, 'but what can we do, sir?', she asks.

The houses on both sides of the metal road show affluence. Walking further down the road, we see a cluster of huts, made of unbaked bricks and thatched roofs. All these huts have kitchens that are separate from the house. The women say it is 'better this way because the smoke will not enter the house'. It is true that smoke will not enter directly into the house. These kitchens have built-in stoves on the floor. There are a few aluminium and clay pots and pans – *congee*[7] being prepared **on** one of the two stoves. They buy wood from the market. They also have a kerosene stove and regularly purchase kerosene from the ration shop. They pour a little bit of kerosene on the wood to speed up the ignition process. All the eight families have ration cards. They do not have electricity, but use hanging kerosene lamps. They also have small medicine bottles filled with kerosene and wick. There is no bathroom, but they have a pit toilet, screened by palm leaves. The circular shaped toilet commode is made of reinforced concrete and beneath the commode is a pit. Since the well has a perennial water supply, they do not have water scarcity. Both men and women take a bath at the side of the well, drawing water straight from the well. There is an abandoned woman, with two children, now being taken care of by her seventy-six year old mother.

The panchayat is full of coconut trees. In one of the small junctions, on the wooden planks of a closed shop, is a Rotary Club poster advertising free polio vaccinations. The interior of the panchayat gives a totally different picture – a picture of deprivation and poverty. As an area develops, poor people sell their land near the road, and move into the interior. Hence a casual visit to the main centres of any Kerala panchayat will hide the micro grass-root level realities. At the same time, there is no despair in the voices of the poor. They are happy, send their children to schools, and hope for a 'better tomorrow'. For example, across the main road, near the paddy fields, lives Abdul Rahman in his beautiful hut, with his nine-month old baby and his wife, who, at the arrival of a stranger immediately disappears. The walls and the roof are made of beautifully woven palm tree leaves. There are two doors, one in the front and one at the back. The house was built recently, costing about Rs. 7,000, and the interior is kept neat and tidy. No bathroom, no toilet, only a well in which the reflection of the mango tree could be seen clearly. A Hercules bicycle is kept in front of the hut. Abdul Rahman is a casual labourer, doing odd jobs. His has one of the happiest faces one could ever see.

Karoor, the high level panchayat

Palai, from where we have to take a bus or an autorikshaw to reach the high-level panchayat, has affluence rarely seen in other Kerala towns. Though the Kerala State Road Transport Corporation bus station is as crowded and as ill-maintained as any other bus station in Kerala, as we step out of the bus station, we see the co-existence of affluence and poverty. Unlike the other Kerala towns or cities, we see youth clad in expensive dhothis and shirts, driving new Maruthi cars. The Indian Coffee House in Palai is crowded with affluent youth. On the sides of the road are beggars, blind and lame, waiting for the mercy of passers-by, who are oblivious to their presence.

In the private bus station, there is high activity level, with employees, colloquially called 'birds', implying the speed with which they hop in and out of the buses, announcing the destinations at the top of their voices. A loud speaker also does the same thing. Even in that confusion, we could not help noticing men urinating behind the pan-shops adjacent to the concrete shelter of the bus stop.

Once inside the crowded bus, you cannot help noticing that the seats reserved for women are occupied by men. They are deliberately oblivious of the fact that women, even mothers with small babies are standing, while they are 'enjoying' the natural scenery through the windows. This is nothing unusual – all over Kerala, we encounter the same situation, where even the 'reservation' of seats in buses for women becomes futile.

In the panchayat, the roads, lanes and bylanes are all dark, the sunlight being blocked by the omnipresent rubber trees. The high-level panchayat is filled with rubber trees of different ages. The lanes and bylanes are deserted. An occasional mother and child on their way to the Meenachal river to take a bath and wash clothes, children playing cricket on the road, a rubber tapper going somewhere, a dignified nun returning to the convent ... an eighty-year old man from the scheduled tribe community, with a beaming smile and all his teeth intact, willing to exchange pleasantries ...

Hidden among the tall rubber trees, we see quite a few concrete houses, with rubber sheets spread out to dry in the sun. The affluent dislike intruders and are suspicious of them.

We see a church and a lower primary school, which as we would imagine, do not have a toilet facility, the well is quite dry and ill-kept and uncared for – even the protective wall is all damaged.

As we walk along, we see a Harijan colony, with houses made of unbaked bricks and thatched roofs. Women and children come out, greet us and despite the visible poverty, assure us that things are fine. They are extremely poor. All of them are casual labourers, mostly engaged in rubber tapping. Even amidst the poverty, all the children in the colony attend school.

Walking along, we reach another housing colony, built by the government under the rural development scheme. There is a public well and two girls, one wearing north Indian churidhar and the other, a long skirt, are drawing water from the well. The man standing nearby explains that there is water in the well because the municipality brings water in tanks and pumps the water into the well. We refuse to believe, considering the fact that it is against basic principles of geology, and quite a substantial amount of water would go to waste, going deep into the soil. But checking with others, we find it is true. The municipality brings water tankers and pumps water into the wells in the panchayats twice a week. The public taps are dry and so are most of the wells. In the high-level panchayat, the diameters of the wells are much larger than those in low-land and mid-land areas.

Near the rubber estates, we see piles of small rubber wood kept by someone to be used as fuel. The saw-mill nearby also sells wood chips and wood dust to poor people. In another junction, we see a reading room and another public well, tea shops and a toddy shop. We see occasional cycles, pedalled by tribals wearing hand-made hats.

In the one lakh housing scheme colony, there is a small pan-shop, selling a few vegetables, coconuts, beedies[8] and fresh lime-juice. Many beneficiaries in the colony have left after selling off their houses. The current market price is Rs. 30,000 per unit. Some of the families have pit toilet facilities, while most do not. Public wells are the main source of drinking water for all the families.

Walking, on what seem like the never-ending roads of the high-level panchayat, a beautiful hut made of grass strikes our attention. Here lives Velan, aged 45, belonging to the scheduled caste. His hut is very small, there is a partition separating the living-cum-bed room from the kitchen. His possessions are few; a couple of iron trunks, a few pots and pans. No well, no electricity and no toilet. Though deprived of tangible possessions, his children go to college. He has studied only up to standard V, but he wants his children to get 'good education'. He strives for that, working day in and day out.

John, the autorikshaw driver, who took us around the panchayat area a couple of times, also spends his hard-earned money on his children's education. In a brick and tiled house in 25 cents of land, he lives with his wife and two children. John also invests in his children's education along with his investments in rubber trees.

Data interpretation

Religion

According to 1991 census, Hindus, Muslims and Christians account for 99.93% of the population in Kerala. Hindus are in the majority (57.28%), followed by Muslims (23.23%) and Christians (19.32%). Apart from Punjab, with its 65.54% of non-Hindu population, Kerala is the only major state in which more than 40% of the population are non-Hindus. As is evident from Table 5.1, the religious composition of our data set matches with the census data.

Though Hindus are in a majority in 11 out of 14 districts, the religious composition of the districts in Kerala varies. These variations are reflected in the survey data (Table 5.2). For example, in the high-level panchayat, Christians constitute 46.57% of the households while Muslims account for only 0.21%. On the other hand, in the mid-level panchayat, Muslims (41.99%) outnumber Christians (2.34%).

Table 5.1   Composition of the population in Kerala by religion (in %)

Religion	Census data	Survey data
Hindus	57.28	59.24
Muslims	23.23	20.93
Christians	19.32	19.28

Sources: *Census of India*, 1991; survey data.

Table 5.2   Families by religion in the panchayats (in %)

Religion	Low-level panchayat	Mid-level panchayat	High-level panchayat	Total
Hindus	70.40	55.07	53.11	59.24
Muslims	22.34	41.99	0.21	20.93
Christians	6.26	2.34	46.57	19.28
Others	0.59	0.46	0.08	0.37
Unknown	0.41	0.14	0.03	0.19
Total	N = 3,389	N = 3,503	N = 3,792	N = 10,684

Social class

Table 5.3   Families by social class in the panchayats (in %)

Social class	Low-level panchayat	Mid-level panchayat	High-level panchayat	Total
Scheduled caste	11.07	16.01	8.89	11.92
Scheduled tribe	0.83	2.37	3.51	2.31
Others	87.75	80.36	87.61	85.25
Unknown	0.35	1.26	0.00	0.52
Total	N = 3,389	N = 3,503	N = 3,792	N = 10,684

According to the 1991 census, the scheduled caste population of Kerala was 2,887,000 constituting 9.92% of the total population. Our sample has 11.92% of scheduled caste households. According to the 1991 census, the scheduled tribe population of Kerala was 320,000, constituting 1.10% of the total population. The sample has 2.31% of households belonging to scheduled tribes.

Housing – ownership

Data shows that the majority – 96.81% of the households own the houses they live in. This is not the case in urban areas, where the land value is very high and a considerable percentage of the population are migrants from rural areas. The urban-rural disparity in tenure status is reflected in the census figures for Kerala. As against 10.18% of the households living in rented houses in urban areas, only 3.24% in rural areas live in rented houses (*Census*, 1991).

The difference in ownership of houses in the three panchayats is not significant. The low-level panchayat has the highest percentage of households living in own houses, followed by the high-level and mid-level panchayats.

Table 5.4   House ownership in the panchayats (in %)

Tenure status	Low-level panchayat	Mid-level panchayat	High-level panchayat	Total
Own	98.05	95.35	97.05	96.81
Rented	1.39	3.60	2.87	2.64
Unknown	0.56	1.06	0.08	0.55
Total	N = 3,389	N = 3,503	N = 3,792	N = 10,684

Type of housing

Irrespective of income levels and the type of housing, houses in Kerala are generally clean. The houses are usually independent, physically separate units, with at least, a little land around. The houses are usually separated by 'compound walls' made of brick/mud/palm leaves or even rows of plants. Though the density of population is high, the average size of the household is 5.3, against the all India figure of 5.6. Hence the extent of overcrowding in the dwellings in Kerala is low compared to the all India scene.

Census data reveal that the housing condition in Kerala, though improving, cannot be termed satisfactory. According to the 1971 census, the total number of households exceeded the number of available houses by 125,000. By 1981, the shortage had increased to 156,000. But by 1991, against the available 5,513,000 houses, there were 5,459,000 households, indicating a need for 54,000 more houses. The reduction in the shortage was due to the high rate of growth of residential buildings during 1981–91 period (27.64%) against a population growth of 14.32%.

But these numbers do not reveal the quality of housing. According to the government of Kerala, about 20% of the existing houses are thatched huts of semi-permanent nature, and 50% of these are substandard huts 'which are not fit for safe human living' In addition, 5% of the existing houses need to be demolished and reconstructed. Thus the housing shortage in Kerala could be estimated to 874,000 (*Economic Review*, 1995).

In 1971, the government of Kerala introduced 'One Lakh Housing scheme'.[9] Though the government failed to achieve full target and the design and the quality of housing left much to be desired, the scheme was a great step forward in solving the housing problem in Kerala.

In Kerala, regional characteristics and the economic status of the family determine the type of material used for walls, and roof. Predominant materials of walls can be classified into: i) grass, leaves, reeds or bamboos; ii) mud; iii) unbaked bricks; iv) wood; v) baked bricks; vi) metal sheets; vii) stone; and viii) cement concrete. The types of material used for roofing are: i) tiles; ii) tin sheets; iii) grass leaves; and iv) concrete.

Though palm leaves are available in plenty, thatched roofs are not cost-effective in Kerala. Every two years, the roofing needs to be changed. Though there have been efforts to extend the longevity of palm leave roofs by chemical processing, it has not been very successful so far. Thus poor people living in houses with thatched roofs incur recurring expenditure for maintenance.

From the 1960s onwards, concrete houses became a symbol of affluence, though not suitable for the tropical climate. Architecture in

Kerala underwent a thorough transformation, replacing the conical roofing with flat roofs, least suitable for the climatic conditions of Kerala. The type of housing reflects the economic status of the Keralite. Mud houses stand lowest in the hierarchy, followed by brickwork and thatched houses. Brickwork and tiled/sheet are considered relatively superior and concrete houses stand highest in the status hierarchy.

Survey data shows that 16.86% of people live in mud constructions and 16.34% in brickwork and thatched houses. Majority of the people live in brickwork and tile/sheet roofed houses (48.79%) and 17.58% live in concrete houses.

Table 5.5   Housing conditions in the panchayats (in %)

Type of house	Low-level panchayat	Mid-level panchayat	High-level panchayat	Total
Mud	26.76	13.67	10.94	16.86
Brickwork and thatched	11.42	31.12	7.09	16.34
Brickwork and tiled/sheet	43.29	32.74	68.54	48.79
Concrete	17.88	21.90	13.32	17.58
Unknown	0.65	0.57	0.11	0.43
Total	N = 3,389	N = 3,503	N = 3,792	N = 10,684

The type of housing varies from region to region in Kerala, as is reflected in the panchayats under study (Table 5.5). If we divide the categories of housing into two – mud, and brickwork and thatched, and brickwork, tiled/sheet and concrete – we will find that the high-level panchayat has better housing facilities (81.86%), followed by the low-level (61.17%) and the mid-level panchayats (51.70%).

Type of stove

Cooking in Kerala is a time-consuming process, involving a lot of wet and dry grinding. Rice is the staple food of Malayalis and tapioca, fish and vegetables form an integral part of Kerala cuisine. The type of stove in use also reflects the economic status of the household. The range of stoves starts from stone-open stoves, where three stones are placed together to make it a stove, to stone side-closed stoves and fuel efficient stoves. Fuel-efficient stoves range from smokeless *choolas* to kerosene stoves. Liquid Petroleum Gas (LPG) cylinder supply is mostly restricted to urban areas and the waiting time for a connection is high.

The aggregate data shows that majority use stoves made of stone, with sides closed (57.3%), followed by users of side open stoves (34.65%). Fuel efficient stoves are used only by a minority – 5.76% and other types of stoves (including electricity, LPG) are used by 0.47% of households.

Table 5.6   Type of cooking stove used in the panchayats (in %)

Type of stove	Low-level panchayat	Mid-level panchayat	High-level panchayat	Total
Stone-open	74.42	20.87	11.84	34.65
Stone-sides closed	13.07	72.62	82.73	57.32
Fuel efficient	7.64	5.05	4.72	5.76
Others	0.50	0.40	0.50	0.47
Unknown	4.37	1.06	0.21	1.81
Total	N = 3,389	N = 3,503	N = 3,792	N = 10,684

But the regional differences in the type of stove used, are remarkable (Table 5.6). For example, in the low-level panchayat, three quarters of households use open stone stoves, followed by less than a quarter of households in the mid-level panchayat and only 12% in the high-level panchayat.

There is a significant difference in the use of stone-sides closed and fuel efficient stoves in these panchayats. But there is no significant difference in the use of other types of stoves, in all these regions.

Type of cooking fuel

People in Kerala use coconut waste, wood, charcoal, kerosene, petroleum gas, electricity and natural gas for cooking. Coconut waste is available in plenty, especially in the low and mid level rural areas. Wood is usually bought from the open market, and hence, except in the tribal belts of Kerala, women do not have the job of collecting fuel. Kerosene, used for both cooking and lighting purposes, is distributed through a very efficient public distribution net work, known as ration shops. Households using electricity as cooking fuel, do not solely depend on electricity – considering the expense involved and the frequent interruptions to electricity supply. Natural gas like bio-gas is not very popular in Kerala.

Table 5.7   Type of cooking fuel used in the panchayats (in %)

Cooking fuel	Low-level panchayat	Mid-level panchayat	High-level panchayat	Total
Coconut waste	57.48	15.10	0.58	23.39
Wood/ Charcoal	4.25	5.31	2.03	3.81
Kerosene	26.73	74.25	92.67	65.72
LPG	0.47	1.26	0.79	0.84
Electricity	7.05	3.08	2.03	3.97
Natural gas	0.03	0.03	0.08	0.05
Others	0.15	0.17	1.61	0.67
Unknown	3.84	0.80	0.21	1.55
Total	N = 3,389	N = 3,503	N = 3,792	N = 10,684

The available data shows that 23.39% of the households use coconut waste as cooking fuel. Wood is used only by 3.81% of the households. It is no surprise, because wood from the open market is expensive. 65.72% of the households under study use kerosene as cooking fuel, and this could be attributed to the steady and effective public distribution of kerosene at subsidized prices. In general, only 0.84% of the households use LPG. But 3.97% of the households use electricity for cooking. A negligible 0.05% use natural gas for cooking.

In reality most of the families might be using more than a single type of cooking fuel. Since the questionnaire had provision for just one entry under this category; it may be assumed that the households have chosen the most used fuel. Hence this information is more suggestive than indicative of fuel usage.

Source of drinking water

Kerala has an average rain fall of 3,000 mm every year, most of it wasted. This is mainly due to the topography, heavy waterflow, soil erosion, closeness to the sea and poor water conservation and management. It is estimated that out of 116,850 million cubic meters of rain water, 70,720 million cubic metres (60%) are lost. The balance is only 42,720 million cubic meters. This means that the state has a deficit of 5,630 million cubic meters of water. To a certain extent, the ground water could be utilised for making good the deficit. Many places in Kerala suffer water scarcity during the summer months of February, March, April and May (interview with Nair).

Government statistics say that 43.75% of the rural population and 64.5% of the urban population have potable drinking water. 5.75% of the households, numbering 464,000, were connected to a piped water supply as on 31.10.1994. Government estimates that every stand pipe (public tap) benefits a population of 250 and as on 31.1.1994, 106,300 stand posts were installed. Government had set the target of 100% coverage of both in rural and urban areas during the sixth five year plan ending in the year 1985 (*State Planning Board: Sixth Five Year Plan*, 1980–85). In a study of rural Kerala by Kerala Sasthra Sahitya Parishad (Kannan, et. al, 1991), it was seen that the incidence of diarrhoea is less among the population using their own wells and tap water at home, and more among those using public wells and public taps. If this study is an indicator, the quality of public tap-water leaves much to be desired.

The government has not even succeeded in providing potable water to all the anganwadis (women's centres). Out of 15,350 anganwadis spread all over the state, only 2,250 anganwadis are provided with water supply facilities (*State Action Plan for Child in Kerala*). Out of 1,384 villages in Kerala, five villages with a total population of 75,597 do not have any source of drinking water.

The drinking water supply system of Kerala can be broadly classified into:

1. River based urban and rural water supply schemes
2. Ground water-based rural water supply schemes
3. Family-managed drinking water systems.

According to the state government, there are 500,000 private wells in Kerala (*Economic Review*, 1994). Citing investigations made by the Centre for Water Resource Development and Management (CWRDM) in 1989, Kurup (1994) argues that Kerala has the highest density of wells in the world. On an average, there are 250 wells per sq. km in low land, 150 in mid-land and 25 in high-land areas. Even today, it is a practice in Kerala to dig a well near the proposed kitchen before starting construction of the house. But lack of toilet facilities, use of pesticides in agriculture and lack of garbage disposal have affected the quality of well water in several areas. A study conducted by the State Pollution Board revealed that 96% of the wells lack the quality specified by the Bureau of Indian Standards for drinking water (Kurup, 1994).

Table 5.8   Source of drinking water in the panchayats (in %)

Source of drinking water	Low-level panchayat	Mid-level panchayat	High-level panchayat	Total
Tap water	7.29	5.00	2.87	4.97
Well/ pond	85.51	82.36	91.82	86.72
Public well/ pond	1.33	9.02	4.72	5.05
River/ Canal	1.30	0.71	0.11	0.68
Others	0.68	0.91	0.08	0.54
Unknown	3.89	2.00	0.40	2.03
Total	N = 3,389	N = 3,503	N = 3,792	N = 10,684

The present study also shows that only 4.97% of the population has access to tap water. 86.72% of the population depend on private well/pond. 5.05% rely on public well/pond. 0.66% of the population under study drink water from river/canal. The highest percentage of tap water users is in the low-level panchayat – 7.29 and lowest in the high-level panchayat – 2.87%. The highest percentage of households using family well/pond is in the high-level panchayat (91.82%).

Scarcity of drinking water

During the summer season, wells dry up, more so in high-land areas. Hence, 57.86% of households in the high-level panchayat feel the scarcity of drinking water. 34.58% of households in the low-level panchayat face scarcity of water. In the mid-level panchayat, this percentage is slightly lower, 23.18%.

Table 5.9   Scarcity of drinking water in the panchayats (in %)

Scarcity of drinking water	Low-level panchayat	Mid-level panchayat	High-level panchayat	Total
Yes	34.58	23.18	57.86	39.11
No	61.70	74.31	41.93	58.82
Unknown	3.72	2.51	0.21	2.08
Total	N = 3,389	N = 3,503	N = 3,792	N = 10,684

Type of toilet

According to data published in *Sarvekshana* (January–March 1992, cited in *Economic Review*, 1994), 51.54% of the households in Kerala have no latrines. Out of the 5,521,000 households, National Sample Survey estimates that about 2,900,000 households are without latrine facilities. According to 1991 census, the sanitation coverage in Kerala is 50.4% with urban households having 72.66% coverage and rural households 42.4% coverage. Only two cities are at least partially covered with water carriage sewer system leading to conventional treatment. On-site disposal systems for disposal of human excreta are used in all other parts of the state. Graff (1993) estimates that:

> out of over 3,000,000 rural households, at best 600,000 actually have some form of man-made sanitation. For the 2,400,000 households without

sanitation at best 20,000 new latrines are available each year, less than one percent ... even less than the natural annual increase of Kerala's population (p. 6).

The *State Plan of Action for The Child* in Kerala has the major goal of 'enhancing the coverage of sanitary facilities from the current level to 66.4% rural household and 86% urban household by the year 2000 AD' (p. 60).

The available panchayat data shows that more than 40% of the households have toilets with septic tanks. 29.02% of the households have toilets without septic tanks, but 28.06 % of the households do not have any man-made toilet facility.

Table 5.10   Sanitation in the panchayats (in %)

Type of toilet	Low-level panchayat	Mid-level panchayat	High-level panchayat	Total
Septic tank	37.89	47.87	34.92	40.11
Without septic tank	32.31	27.43	27.53	29.02
Open space	24.76	21.44	37.13	28.06
Unknown	5.05	3.25	0.42	2.82
Total	N = 3,389	N = 3,503	N = 3,792	N = 10,684

It may be noted from Table 5.10 that sanitation aspects in the mid-level panchayat are slightly better. In the high-level panchayat, a very high percentage of households lack any man-made toilet facility. This may be due to the availability of more open space in the high-level panchayat.

Needless to say, the absence of man-made toilets makes life extremely difficult for the people of densely populated Kerala. As Indira Gandhi, the late Prime Minister, in one of her communications to Chief Ministers, wrote 'Women specially feel miserable. They can go out for defecation only at night ...' (cited in Kurup, 1993; p. 25). Lack of sanitation facilities leads to contamination of surface soil, rivers and backwaters. It will also adversely affect the quality of spring water and well water. This results in high morbidity, especially, for children.

Main source of income

The primary sector contributed 36.66% of the state domestic product. The secondary sector's share was 23.50% and that of the tertiary sector, 39.84%. Though sectoral analysis of income is not available from the survey, the pattern of main source of income could be understood from Table 5.11.

Self-employment is highest in the high-level panchayat, where the primary sector is strong (48.66%) and lowest in the mid-level panchayat (15.67%). Salaried/permanent coolies are highest in the mid-level panchayat (20.44%) and lowest in the low-level panchayat (10.33%). Temporary job holders and temporary coolies form 48.70% among the heads of households in the mid-level panchayat, followed by 39.48% in the low-level panchayat. In the high-level panchayat, only 29.80% of the heads of families are temporary job holders/temporary coolies. Among these panchayats, money from abroad flows most to the mid-level panchayat, with 9.19% of the households depending on foreign remittances, and least to the high-level panchayat, 1.61%.

Table 5.11   Main source of income of households in the panchayats (in %)

Main source of income	Low-level panchayat	Mid-level panchayat	High-level panchayat	Total
Self-employment	38.27	15.67	48.66	34.55
Salary/permanent coolie	10.33	20.44	14.03	14.96
Temporary job/temp. coolie	39.48	48.70	29.80	39.07
Money from abroad	5.78	9.19	1.61	5.42
Others	1.71	0.20	4.09	2.06
Unknown	4.43	5.80	1.82	3.95
Total	N = 3,389	N = 3,503	N = 3,792	N = 10,684

Household industry

Household industries are not common in Kerala, as is evident from the low percentage (4.57%) of industries attached to households in these panchayats (Table 5.12). According to the 1991 census, only 2.58% of the population were engaged in any household industry. There is no significant variation between these panchayats, and the low-level panchayat has a slight edge over other panchayats with 5.37% against 4.22% in the high-level and 4.17% in the mid-level panchayats.

Table 5.12   Household industry in the panchayats (in %)

Household industry	Low-level panchayat	Mid-level panchayat	High-level panchayat	Total
Yes	5.37	4.17	4.22	4.57
No	92.42	88.95	95.65	92.43
Unknown	2.21	6.88	0.13	3.00
Total	N = 3,389	N = 3,503	N = 3,792	N = 10,684

Provision of electricity

Table 5.13   Access to electricity and possession of consumer durables in the panchayats (in %)

Items	Low-level panchayat	Mid-level panchayat	High-level panchayat	Total
Electricity	55.71	69.37	67.80	64.48
Telephone	2.10	1.48	3.14	2.27
Radio	57.30	49.76	69.62	59.20
Television	13.16	24.86	27.03	21.92
Mixie	16.38	16.64	20.44	17.91
Refrigerator	7.88	8.19	12.84	12.55
Washing machine	1.30	1.03	2.56	1.66
Pressure cooker	7.11	4.60	10.63	7.53
Grinder	3.84	4.14	6.78	4.98
Cycle	32.34	27.75	7.44	22.00
Scooter/ Motor cycle	4.96	5.65	5.20	5.27
Car/Jeep	1.74	1.91	2.29	1.99
Total number of households	N = 3,389	N = 3,503	N = 3,792	N = 10,684

In Kerala, electricity is a state monopoly, provided by the Kerala State Electricity Board. Shortage of power continues to be a serious bottleneck for the overall development of the state. Since Kerala relies on hydro-electric power, there is a power shortage every summer and the Electricity Board imposes power cuts during the day time and early evenings during summer. Census data for 1991 reveals that electricity is available to 48.43% of the households in Kerala. Our data shows that 64.48% of the households in all the three panchayats have electricity connection.

Access to possessions

Table 5.13 shows that majority of the population in all the three panchayats do not have much in terms of possessions. Only 59.20% of the population possess even a relatively inexpensive item like a radio. The survey revealed that more households in the high-level panchayat possess domestic gadgets and motorised vehicles when compared to the other two panchayats. Being a low-land area, more households in the low-level panchayat own bicycles (32.34%) and being a high-land area, few households in the high-level panchayat possess bicycles (7.44%).

Ownership of land

Table 5.14   Land ownership in the panchayats (in %)

Land owned	Low-level panchayat	Mid-level panchayat	High-level panchayat
0 cents*	8.46	2.48	3.51
1–4 cents	10.42	9.05	9.73
5–9 cents	19.21	22.89	8.76
10–19 cents	23.96	25.21	13.92
20–49 cents	22.90	26.66	14.24
50–99 cents	9.18	9.82	10.60
100–149 cents	3.07	2.03	8.73
150–199 cents	1.33	0.71	5.46
200–299 cents	0.94	0.86	8.73
300+ cents	0.53	0.29	16.32

Key: * 1 cent is 1% of an acre.

The low-level panchayat has an area of 10.64 sq.km., mid-level panchayat has 13.96 sq.km. and the high level panchayat has 36.84 sq.km. of area. Thus the highest density of population is in the low-level panchayat, followed by mid-level and high-level panchayats respectively. The percentage of landless is the highest in low-level panchayat (8.47%) and lowest in mid-level panchayat (2.48%). More households in the high-level panchayat (49.84%) have more than 50 cents of land, while only 15.04% of households in the low-level panchayat and 13.71% in the mid-level panchayat have more than 50 cents. A considerable percentage of families in the high-level panchayat have more than 300 cents of land (16.32%).

The above analysis reveal that there is wide variation in access to facilities and possessions between the panchayats. But like GNP, these figures show only the wealth (and the relative absence of it) in the three panchayats and reveal nothing about the distribution pattern. In the next section, the data is disaggregated to find out how the 'wealth' is distributed in the three panchayats.

Section Two: Analysis of poverty/affluence

In this section the living standards of the households in the three panchayats are analyzed. This would give a picture of the incidence of poverty in these panchayats in both absolute and relative terms. The inter-regional differences in the standard of living and the differences in the intensity of poverty between these regions have also been assessed.

An aggregate score is arrived at for each family by giving different scores to the set of parameters that have a direct bearing on the level of standard of living of the people. The scores assigned vary from 0 to 30 depending on the parameter and its economic significance. Those items that are perceived as prestige items in Kerala society – like washing machines and cars are given high scores, and those which are perceived as essential, are given low scores.

The scores given are adapted from a paper (Sidharthan et. al, 1995) on peoples' resource mapping programme in the state. The scores ascribed to the various items are specific to Kerala society and cannot be considered as holding good in other societies/economies. Care has been taken to ascribe scores based on a need hierarchy in the Kerala context. This need-hierarchy has basis on the living styles and aspirations of the society being studied. Thus the parameters include various aspects of family; ranging from structure, to facilities and possessions enjoyed by the families. A composite index of standard of living has been arrived at, by aggregating the scores on the various items.

The exhaustive nature of this micro-level data permits us to evaluate the quality of life of the people in these panchayats. Similar data are not available at the macro-level for the state as a whole. Though the scores assigned could be argued to be subjective, it could be safely assumed that the scores are a near true reflection of the socio-economic reality of the various families.

The values assigned to the different parameters are given in Table 5.15. For the purpose of analysis, families with an aggregate score of 0–25 are considered poor and among this group, families scoring less than 10 are treated as very poor. Those families with scores ranging from 25–100 are considered middle-class and families with more than 100 scores are treated as belonging to the upper class.

Table 5.15   Scores for facilities and possessions of households

Items	Scores
House type	
Mud	0
Brick work and thatched	2
Brick work and tiled/sheet	4
Concrete	8
Stove type	
Stone-open	0
Stone-sides closed	1
Fuel efficient	3
LPG, bio-gas, electricity	10
Cooking fuel	
Coconut waste	0
Wood/Charcoal	1
Kerosene	2
LPG, bio-gas, electricity	10

Source of drinking water

Other public sources	0
Own well/pond	1
Tap water	3

Toilet type

Others	0
Without septic tank	3
Septic tank	5

Main source of income

Temporary job/temp. coolie	1
Self-employment	2
Salary/permanent coolie	2
Others	2
Foreign remittances	10

Facilities/Possessions

Electricity	1
Radio	1
Cycle	1
Mixie	5
Pressure cooker	6
Wet grinder	6
Television	12
Refrigerator	12
Scooter/Motor cycle	12
Washing machine	18
Telephone	30
Car/Jeep	30

Land possessed*

0 cents	0
1–4 cents	1
>4, <10	2
>9, <20	4
>19, < 50	6
>49, < 100	8
> 99, < 150	12
>149, < 200	16
> 199, < 300	24

> 299	48
< 5	0
6	−1
7	−2
8	−3
9	−4
10	−5
above 10	−6

Key: One cent is 1% of an acre.

The results of Chi square tests of significance to assess the relationship between the level of poverty and other variables are also given in this section.

Poverty and affluence in the low-level panchayat (Krishnapuram)

Of the 3,389 families in the low-level panchayat, 809 families are very poor, 1,764 families, poor, 747 families fall under the category of middle-class and 69 families are rich.

Figure 5.1   Profile of poverty/affluence in the low-level panchayat

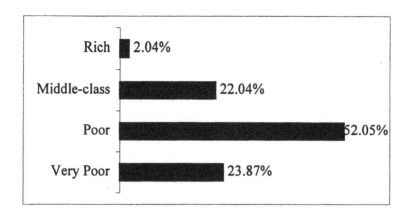

Family size

The average size of the family in the low-level panchayat is 4.97, a figure, lower than the state average of 5.30. Very poor households have a family size of 5.33, poor families, 4.89, middle class families, 4.73 and rich families, 5.26. Both very poor and rich households have more family members, as revealed by their mean family size.

Figure 5.2   Family size in the low-level panchayat

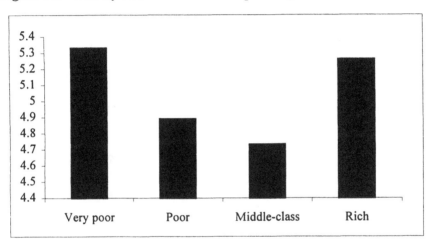

Main source of income

Table 5.16   Main source of income of households in the low-level panchayat (in %)

Categories	Temp. job	Permanent job	Foreign remittance	Total
Very poor	60.07	29.05	0.00	N = 809
Poor	40.93	52.27	4.31	N = 1,764
Middle-class	16.34	66.13	15.26	N = 647
Rich	11.59	78.26	8.70	N = 69
Total	39.48	50.31	5.78	N = 3,389

Chi square test value = 2.14237E-17; significant at $p < 0.01$

The relationship between the main source of income and the level of poverty/affluence is clear from Table 5.16. Majority of the very poor does not have a permanent job, while majority of middle-income and rich households has income from permanent jobs.

Housing conditions

The housing conditions of majority of very poor households are far from satisfactory. Only 14.22% have relatively better housing – walls made of bricks and tiled/sheet roofing and concrete. Majority of the middle class and rich live in better houses.

Table 5.17   Housing conditions in the low-level panchayat (in %)

Categories	Mud	Brick work and thatched	Brick work and tiled/sheet	Concrete	Total
Very poor	73.79	10.14	13.60	0.62	N = 809
Poor	16.84	15.70	56.52	10.71	N = 1,764
Middle-class	1.47	3.34	46.72	48.06	N = 747
Rich	2.90	4.35	15.94	76.81	N = 69
Total	26.76	11.42	43.29	17.88	N = 3,389

Chi square test value = 1.78668E-61; significant at p < 0.01

Sanitation

Table 5.18   Sanitation in the low-level panchayat (in %)

Categories	Open	Without septic tank	With septic tank	Total
Very poor	69.10	14.46	4.82	N = 809
Poor	14.91	45.98	35.83	N = 1,764
Middle-class	2.28	21.69	73.63	N = 747
Rich	0.00	7.25	91.30	N = 69
Total	24.76	32.31	37.89	N = 3,389

Chi square test value = 2.59677E-57; significant at p < 0.01

Social stratification

An analysis of the relationship between social classes and standard of living reveals that the previously oppressed classes still remain in poverty. 95.73% of the scheduled castes and 92.85% of scheduled tribes are either very poor or poor.

Table 5.19   Social stratification and economic classification in the low-level panchayat (in %)

Categories	Scheduled caste	Scheduled tribe	General
Very poor	42.13	32.14	21.50
Poor	53.60	60.71	51.77
Middle-class	4.00	7.14	24.45
Rich	0.27	0.00	2.28
Total	N = 375	N = 28	N = 2,974

Chi square test value = 1.97125E-05; significant at $p < 0.01$

Source of drinking water

Though Table 5.20 shows that majority of all classes of people have their own wells, the quality of water is obviously not reflected in the data. Considering the environmental factors, it could be said that the rich man's well is superior to the poor man's well. Though the data shows that a considerable percentage of very poor and poor people use tap water, they rely on public taps. Only the affluent in the panchayat has tap water at home.

Table 5.20   Source of drinking water in the low-level panchayat (in %)

Categories	Own well	Tap water	Public sources	Total
Very poor	75.90	5.19	9.52	N = 809
Poor	91.55	4.48	1.81	N = 1,764
Middle-class	83.00	14.32	0.27	N = 747
Rich	71.01	27.54	1.45	N = 69
Total	85.51	7.29	3.31	N = 3,389

Chi square test value = 2.88039E-08; significant at $p < 0.01$

Type of cooking fuel

The low level panchayat has plenty of coconut trees. As would be expected, the majority of the very poor and poor, depend on coconut waste for fuel, while the rich use LPG/electricity as their main cooking fuel. All classes of households buy kerosene from the ration shops.

Table 5.21 Types of cooking fuel used in the low-level panchayat (in %)

Categories	Coconut waste	Wood/ Charcoal	Kerosene	LPG/ Electricity	Total
Very poor	69.34	1.85	18.91	0.00	N = 809
Poor	61.90	6.24	29.59	0.28	N = 1,764
Middle-class	38.29	2.41	30.25	27.31	N = 747
Rich	13.04	1.45	7.25	75.36	N = 69
Total	57.48	4.25	26.73	7.55	N = 3,389

Chi square test value = 2.76818E-40; significant at $p < 0.01$

Type of stove

Table 5.22 Types of cooking stove used in the low-level panchayat (in %)

Categories	Stone -open	Stone- sides closed	Fuel efficient	LPG/ Electricity	Total
Very poor	82.08	7.29	0.12	0.00	N = 809
Poor	77.95	18.20	1.30	0.06	N = 1,764
Middle-class	62.52	8.30	25.03	1.87	N = 747
Rich	23.19	1.45	69.57	2.90	N = 69
Total	74.42	13.07	7.64	0.50	N = 3,389

Chi square test value = 1.53068E-35; significant at $p < 0.01$

Though the data differentiates between different stoves, in reality, the same households will be using different types of stoves. But since the poor and very poor cannot afford fuel-efficient and modern stoves, and the recurring costs involved, the majority of them rely on stone-open and stone-sides closed stoves.

Electricity

The data shows that only a minority (12.86%) of the very poor families have electricity and during the visits to the panchayats, it was observed that even among those households that have electricity, they have only one electric point, with a 15V/25V light bulb. Only the middle class and the rich, the majority of whom, have electricity at home, have sufficient electric points.

Table 5.23   Access to electricity in the low-level panchayat (in %)

Categories	Families with electricity	Total no. of families
Very poor	12.86	N = 809
Poor	56.97	N = 1,764
Middle-class	95.31	N = 747
Rich	97.10	N = 69
Total	55.71	N = 3,389

Ownership of land

It is discernible from Table 5.24 that only a minority of the very poor (20.64%) have an electrical home appliance like a radio. Even in low-land, where cycling is easier, the very poor cannot afford bicycles. The table shows that the higher the income-strata, the greater the level of affluence. Since the majority of the scheduled castes and scheduled tribes fall into the categories of very poor and poor (Table 5.19), it could be argued that the lower the social class, lower is their economic strata.

Disaggregated analysis of ownership of land shows that the majority of the very poor, poor and middle-class have less than 50 cents of land in their possession. A greater number of families in the middle-class and rich brackets have more than 50 cents of land (40.43% of middle-class and 57.97% of rich households). A fairly high percentage (34.78%) of rich households have more than one acre of land.

Possessions

Table 5.24   Possession of consumer durables in the low-level panchayat (in %)

Categories	Radio	TV	Mixie	Fridge	Pressure cooker	Grinder	Total no. of families
Very poor	20.64	0.00	0.00	0.00	0.00	0.00	N = 809
Poor	57.99	7.37	2.89	0.00	0.17	0.17	N = 1,764
Middle-class	91.43	49	58.10	26.77	24.36	11.51	N = 747
Rich	100	97.0	100	97.10	81.16	71.01	N = 69
Total	57.30	13.16	16.38	7.88	7.11	3.84	N = 3,389

Categories	Washing Machine	Cycle	Scooter	Car/Jeep	Phone	Total no. of families
Very poor	0.00	11.50	0.00	0.00	0.00	N = 809
Poor	0.00	30.61	0.30	0.00	0.00	N = 1,764
Middle-class	2.14	54.62	15.53	2.68	2.81	N = 747
Rich	40.58	79.71	66.67	56.52	72.46	N = 69
Total	1.30	32.34	4.96	1.74	2.10	N = 3,389

Chi square test value = 4.22384E-56; significant at $p < 0.01$

Table 5.25 Possession of land in the low-level panchayat (in %)

Extent of land (in cents)	Very poor	Poor	Middle-class	Rich	Total
0	15.20	5.78	7.63	7.25	8.46
1–5	36.96	13.15	4.15	10.14	16.79
6–10	28.68	21.43	5.62	0.00	19.23
11–50	19.04	51.87	42.17	24.64	41.33
51–100	0.12	7.14	22.09	23.19	9.09
Above 100	0.00	0.62	18.34	34.78	5.07
Total no. of families	N = 809	N = 1764	N = 747	N = 69	N = 3389

Key: 1 cent is 1% of an acre.
Chi square test value = 3.18575E-33; significant at p < 0.01

Poverty and affluence in the mid-level panchayat (Andoorkonam)

Figure 5.3 Profile of poverty/affluence in the mid-level panchayat

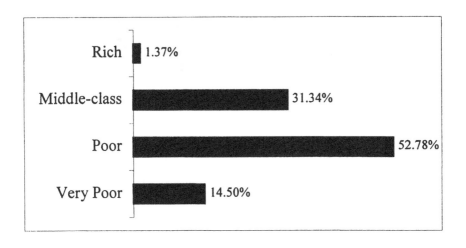

Of the 3,503 families in the mid-level panchayat of Andoorkonam, 508 families are very poor, 1,849 families, poor, 1,098 families fall into the category of middle-class; and 48 families are rich.

Family size

The average size of the family in the mid-level panchayat is 4.82 a figure, lower than the state average of 5.30. Very poor households have a family size of 5.08, poor families, 4.87, middle class families, 4.61 and rich families, 5.06. Both very poor and rich households have more family members as revealed by their mean family size.

Figure 5.4   Family size in the mid-level panchayat

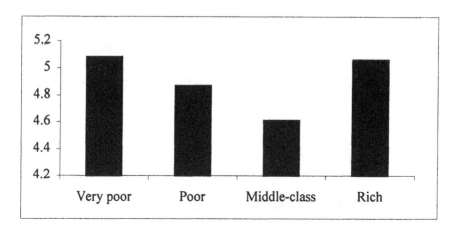

Main source of income

We can discern from Table 5.26 that majority of very poor people (75.98%) rely on temporary jobs, mostly as casual labourers or coolies. A high percentage of middle class (51.00) and rich (60.42) have permanent jobs. Foreign remittance has a direct impact on the economic situation of the households, as is reflected in the middle class and rich categories.

Table 5.26   Main source of income of households in the mid-level panchayat (in %)

Categories	Temp. job	Permanent job	Foreign remittance	Total
Very poor	75.98	16.73	0.00	N = 508
Poor	55.16	32.83	6.06	N = 1,849
Middle-class	26.59	51.00	18.40	N = 1,098
Rich	16.67	60.42	16.67	N = 48
Total	48.70	36.31	9.19	N = 3,503

Chi square test value = 1.30472E-19; significant at $p < 0.01$

Housing conditions

It is evident from Table 5.27 that economic conditions of the households are reflected in the type of housing. While the majority of the middle class and the rich live in either concrete or brickwork and tiled/sheet roof houses, the majority of the very poor live in mud houses and poor in brickwork and thatched houses.

Table 5.27   Housing conditions in the mid-level panchayat (in %)

Categories	Mud	Brick work and thatched	Brick work and tiled/sheet	Concrete	Total
Very poor	35.04	44.69	18.11	0.20	N = 508
Poor	14.49	40.78	37.59	6.65	N = 1,849
Middle-class	3.01	9.84	32.33	54.92	N = 1,098
Rich	0.00	2.08	10.42	85.42	N = 48
Total	13.67	31.12	32.74	21.90	N = 3,503

Chi square test value = 8.10397E-53; significant at $p < 0.01$

Sanitation

The sad state of sanitation in the mid-level panchayat is reflected in Table 5.28. Nearly one fourth of the population uses open spaces as toilets. The majority of the very poor households (75.39%) and a considerable percentage of the poor (17.96%) do not have any man-made toilet facility. It may be noticed that majority of the middle-class and rich households have pit toilets or toilets with septic tanks.

Table 5.28   Sanitation in the mid-level panchayat (in %)

Categories	Open	Without septic tank	With septic tank	Total
Very poor	75.39	13.19	1.38	N = 508
Poor	17.96	36.94	42.24	N = 1,849
Middle-class	3.28	18.49	77.32	N = 1,098
Rich	0.00	16.67	83.33	N = 48
Total	21.44	27.43	47.87	N = 3,503

Chi square test value = 2.12032E-53; significant at $p < 0.01$

Social stratification

It is evident from Table 5.29 that social strata determine the economic strata. More than 90% of the scheduled caste and over 80% of the scheduled tribe remain either very poor or poor and none of them belong to the rich strata.

Table 5.29   Social stratification and economic classification in the mid-level panchayat (in %)

Categories	Scheduled caste	Scheduled tribe	General
Very poor	40.46	12.05	9.34
Poor	52.23	71.08	52.61
Middle-class	7.31	16.87	36.34
Rich	0.00	0.00	1.71
Total	N = 561	N = 83	N = 2,815

Chi square test value = 1.19771E-10; significant at $p < 0.01$

Source of drinking water

In the mid-level panchayat a considerable percentage of the very poor families rely on public sources of water (43.50%). In this panchayat also, the classification of tap water is slightly misleading. The very poor and poor use public stand taps, while the middle-class and the rich households have their own taps inside their houses.

Table 5.30 Source of drinking water in the mid-level panchayat (in %)

Categories	Own well	Tap water	Public sources	Total
Very poor	47.44	3.35	43.50	N = 508
Poor	86.32	4.43	7.52	N = 1,849
Middle-class	91.53	6.47	1.18	N = 1,098
Rich	89.58	10.42	0.00	N = 48
Total	82.36	5.00	10.64	N = 3,503

Chi square test value = 8.89602E-24; significant at $p < 0.01$

Types of cooking fuel

Table 5.31 clearly shows the relationship between poverty and the type of fuel used for cooking. A very high percentage of the very poor in the mid-level panchayat use coconut waste as fuel, but none of these 508 households in the mid-level panchayat use LPG/electricity. During the visit to the mid-level panchayat, it was found that even families who use kerosene use it primarily for making tea or boiling water and they rely mostly on coconut waste for cooking their main meals. They also use kerosene for lighting lamps. The majority (76.05%) of the middle class use kerosene and a high percentage of the rich (56.25%) use LPG/electricity as fuel.

Table 5.31 Types of cooking fuel used in the mid-level panchayat (in %)

Categories	Coconut waste	Wood/ Charcoal	Kerosene	LPG/ Electricity	Total
Very poor	42.91	6.30	48.43	0.00	N = 508
Poor	13.25	5.08	81.12	0.05	N = 1,849
Middle-class	6.01	5.37	76.05	11.93	N = 1,098
Rich	0.00	2.08	41.67	56.25	N = 48
Total	15.10	5.31	74.25	4.37	N = 3,503

Chi square test value = 1.23898E-41; significant at $p < 0.01$

Types of stove

In the mid-level panchayat, some very poor and poor families have their kitchen outside their huts. Those using open stoves use them outside the house. The fact that the numbers of fuel-efficient stove users are so low among the first three categories corroborates the observation that the families in these classes mostly use kerosene for ignition purposes, and they mostly use coconut waste or wood as their main fuel.

Table 5.32   Types of cooking stove used in the mid-level panchayat (in %)

Categories	Stone-open	Stone-sides closed	Fuel efficient	LPG/ Electricity	Total
Very poor	56.89	40.75	0.20	0.00	N = 508
Poor	19.20	78.10	2.00	0.05	N = 1,849
Middle-class	7.83	78.96	11.11	1.00	N = 1,098
Rich	2.08	54.17	35.42	4.17	N = 48
Total	20.87	72.62	5.05	0.40	N =3,503

Chi square test value = 2.90702E-33; significant at $p < 0.01$

Electricity

We can see from Table 5.33 that the majority (70.28%) of the very poor households does not have electricity, while majority of the middle class (98.18%) and all the rich households do.

Table 5.33   Access to electricity in the mid-level panchayat (in %)

Categories	Families with electricity	Total no. of families
Very poor	29.72	508
Poor	62.36	1,849
Middle-class	98.18	1,098
Rich	100.00	48
Total	69.37	3,503

Possessions

Table 5.34   Possession of consumer durables in the mid-level panchayat (in %)

Categories	Radio	TV	Mixie	Fridge	Pressure cooker	Grinder	Total no. of families
Very poor	10.04	0.00	0.00	0.00	0.00	0.00	N = 508
Poor	40.56	1.51	1.78	0.00	0.00	0.00	N = 1,849
Middle-class	81.88	72.40	46.08	22.04	11.75	10.47	N = 1,098
Rich	89.58	100	91.67	93.75	66.67	62.50	N = 48
Total	49.76	24.86	16.64	8.19	4.60	4.14	N = 3,503

Categories	Washing Machine	Cycle	Scooter	Car/Jeep	Phone	Total no. of families
Very poor	0.00	4.72	0.00	0.00	0.00	N = 508
Poor	0.00	20.01	0.11	0.00	0.00	N = 1,849
Middle-class	0.91	50.00	15.48	3.01	1.73	N = 1,098
Rich	54.17	60.42	54.17	70.83	68.75	N = 48
Total	1.03	27.75	5.65	1.91	1.48	N = 3,503

Chi square test value = 4.47747E-52; significant at $p < 0.01$

The very poor and the poor in the mid-level panchayat are deprived of almost all the possessions listed. As in the low-level panchayat, only a minority (10.04%) of the households possess even a radio. At the same time, more than 50% of the rich households have all the items listed in the questionnaire.

Table 5.35 reveals that majority of the very poor have less than 5 cents of land, while majority of the poor and the middle-class have more than 10 cents of land.

Ownership of land

Table 5.35   Possession of land in the mid-level panchayat (in %)

Extent of land (in cents)	Very poor	Poor	Middle-class	Rich	Total
0	4.13	2.70	1.28	4.17	2.48
1-5	55.91	18.23	5.01	2.08	19.33
6-10	24.61	26.28	12.20	2.08	21.30
11-50	15.35	46.51	58.47	45.83	45.73
51-100	0.00	5.95	15.30	16.67	8.16
Above 100	0.00	0.32	7.74	29.17	3.00
Total no. of families	N = 508	N = 1,849	N = 1,098	N = 48	N = 3,503

Key: 1 cent is 1% of an acre.
Chi square test value = 1.08102E-38; significant at $p < 0.01$

Poverty and affluence in the high-level panchayat (Karoor)

Of the 3,792 families in the high-level panchayat of Karoor, 386 families are very poor, 1,704 families, poor, 1,456 families fall under the category of middle-class; and 246 families are rich.

Figure 5.5   Profile of poverty/affluence in the high-level panchayat

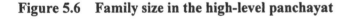

Rich	6.49%
Middle-class	38.40%
Poor	4.93%
Very Poor	10.18%

Family size

The average size of the family in the high-level panchayat is 4.92, a figure lower than the state average of 5.30. Very poor households have a family size of 5.09, poor families, 4.77, middle class families, 4.92 and rich families, 5.68. Both very poor and rich households have more family members as revealed by their mean family size.

Figure 5.6   Family size in the high-level panchayat

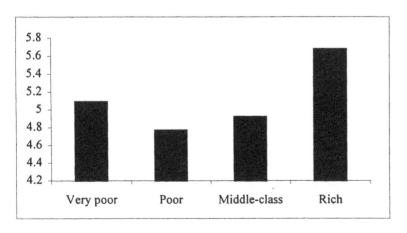

Main source of income

In the high-level panchayat also, poverty and main source of income are highly related. The majority of the very poor have temporary jobs, while only a negligible percentage of the middle-income and rich families depend on temporary jobs as their main source of income. 2% of the poor households have inward foreign remittance. Generally, foreign remittance results in economic mobility of the households – but the number of years of continuous inward remittance and the nature of employment of the family members abroad, are factors that make a significant impact on the economic condition of the households.

Table 5.36   Main source of income of households in the high-level panchayat (in %)

Categories	Temp. job	Permanent job	Foreign remittance	Total
Very poor	77.20	18.91	0.00	N = 386
Poor	44.60	51.58	2.00	N = 1,704
Middle-income	4.60	92.31	1.65	N = 1,456
Rich	2.03	95.93	1.22	N = 246
Total	29.80	66.77	1.61	N = 3,792

Chi square test value = 3.11651E-37; significant at $p < 0.01$

Housing conditions

In the high-level panchayat, the majority of poor families live in mud houses and the majority of poor and middle-class live in houses with walls made of bricks and roofs made of tiles (Table 5.37). This does not mean that the quality of housing of the poor and middle-class are comparable. The size of dwelling of the poor is smaller than that of the middle-class and the quality of construction is, as would be expected, inferior. It is surprising that 2% of poor families live in concrete houses. On verifying the data entries, it is found that these families have foreign remittance as their main source of income (Table 5.36). This reflects the attitudes of Keralites, especially of those who go abroad, to housing. They give priority to housing and the moment they have savings, they invest in building houses.

Table 5.37   Housing conditions in the high-level panchayat (in %)

Categories	Mud	Brick work and thatched	Brick work and tiled/sheet	Concrete	Total
Very poor	67.88	18.39	13.47	0.00	N = 386
Poor	7.39	10.50	80.05	2.00	N = 1,704
Middle-class	1.85	1.20	75.14	21.84	N = 1,456
Rich	0.00	1.22	36.18	62.20	N = 246
Total	10.94	7.09	68.54	13.32	N = 3,792

Chi square test value = 1.24865E-73; significant at $p < 0.01$

Sanitation

The rubber plantations in the high-level panchayat make it relatively easy for the very poor and poor people to use open spaces as toilets. This may be the reason why more households belonging to the middle-class (7.62%) in this panchayat use open space for attending nature's calls when compared to their counterparts in the other two panchayats. As in other panchayats, the majority of the rich in the high-level panchayat too have better sanitation facility.

Table 5.38   Sanitation in the high-level panchayat (in %)

Categories	Open	Without septic tank	With septic tank	Total
Very poor	96.89	1.55	1.04	N = 386
Poor	54.17	27.64	17.78	N = 1,704
Middle-class	7.62	35.71	56.39	N = 1,456
Rich	0.00	19.11	79.67	N = 246
Total	37.13	27.53	34.92	N = 3,792

Chi square test value = 2.72507E-58; significant at $p < 0.01$

Social stratification

In the high-level panchayat also, social class determines the level of poverty/affluence. While only 8.07% of the general population is being classified as very poor, 24.03% of scheduled castes and 27.82% of the scheduled tribes are very poor. The percentage of poor is also high among these two categories (67.95% and 62.41% in the scheduled caste and scheduled tribe, against 41.90% in the general population).

Table 5.39　Social stratification and economic classification in the high-level panchayat (in %)

Categories	Scheduled caste	Scheduled tribe	General
Very poor	24.03	27.82	8.07
Poor	67.95	62.41	41.90
Middle-class	7.72	9.02	42.69
Rich	0.30	0.75	7.34
Total	N = 337	N = 133	N = 3,322

Chi square test value = 8.91256E-13; significant at $p < 0.01$

Source of drinking water

Though majority of all classes of households in the high-level panchayat have their own wells, the scarcity of water during the summer is acute. All wells dry up, but the public wells are more vulnerable as there are more people drawing water from panchayat wells. But the panchayat, with the help of Palai Municipality is regularly taking steps to ensure steady water supply.

Table 5.40　Source of drinking water in the high-level panchayat (in %)

Categories	Own well	Tap water	Public sources	Total
Very poor	81.09	0.78	17.10	N = 386
Poor	91.08	3.64	5.05	N = 1,704
Middle-class	94.57	2.82	2.34	N = 1,456
Rich	97.56	1.22	0.00	N = 246
Total	91.82	2.87	4.91	N = 3,792

Chi square test value = 1.2171E-05; significant at $p < 0.01$

Types of cooking fuel

Coconut trees are rare in the high-level panchayat because it is a rubber plantation area. Hence coconut waste is not available to the poorer sections of the population to be used as fuel. The poorer people of this panchayat, in reality, use waste from old rubber trees. The consumption of kerosene is highest in this panchayat. The majority of middle-class and rich people use kerosene as a major cooking fuel.

Table 5.41   Types of cooking fuel used in the high-level panchayat (in %)

Categories	Coconut waste	Wood/ Charcoal	Kerosene	LPG/ Electricity	Total
Very poor	0.00	2.07	96.89	0.00	N = 386
Poor	0.59	1.88	97.01	0.18	N = 1,704
Middle-class	0.82	2.40	90.11	4.26	N = 1,456
Rich	0.00	0.81	70.73	18.29	N = 246
Total	0.58	2.03	92.67	2.90	N = 3,792

Chi square test value = 2.36215E-07; significant at $p < 0.01$

Types of stove

A very high percentage of the households in the high-level panchayat use stone-sides closed stoves (82.73%). Even among the middle-class and rich households, only a minority (0.89% and 1.63% respectively) use LPG or electricity as fuel.

Table 5.42   Types of cooking stove used in the high-level panchayat (in %)

Categories	Stone-open	Stone-sides closed	Fuel efficient	LPG/ Electricity	Total
Very poor	51.81	46.37	0.78	0.00	N = 386
Poor	12.79	84.98	2.05	0.12	N = 1,704
Middle-class	1.92	90.66	6.39	0.89	N = 1,456
Rich	1.22	76.83	19.51	1.63	N = 246
Total	11.84	82.73	4.72	0.50	N =3,792

Chi square test value = 8.52598E-28; significant at p < 0.01

Electricity

While the majority of the very poor households (91.19%) in this panchayat do not have electricity, the majority of the middle-class and rich people do have electricity (94.37% and 98.78% respectively). Among the three panchayats, the percentage of very poor and poor households with electricity is the lowest in the high-level panchayat (in the low level panchayat, 12.86% of very poor and 56.97% of poor households have electricity; in the mid-level panchayat, 29.72% of the very poor and 62.36% of the poor households have electricity).

Table 5.43   Access to electricity in the high-level panchayat (in %)

Categories	% of families with electricity	Total no. of families
Very poor	8.81	N = 386
Poor	53.93	N = 1,704
Middle-class	94.37	N = 1,456
Rich	98.78	N = 246
Total	67.80	N = 3,972

Possessions

Table 5.44 Possession of consumer durables in the high-level panchayat (in %)

Categories	Radio	TV	Mixie	Fridge	Pressure cooker	Grinder	Total no. of families
Very poor	20.98	0.00	0.00	0.00	0.00	0.00	N = 386
Poor	58.57	0.23	0.41	0.06	0.00	0.18	N = 1,704
Middle-class	90.80	53.85	37.09	17.86	14.90	8.17	N = 1,456
Rich	96.75	95.93	92.68	91.46	75.20	54.47	N = 246
Total	69.62	27.03	20.44	12.84	10.63	6.78	N = 3,792

Categories	Washing Machine	Cycle	Scooter	Car/Jeep	Phone	Total no. of families
Very poor	0.00	0.52	0.00	0.00	0.00	N = 386
Poor	0.00	2.46	0.00	0.00	0.00	N = 1,704
Middle-class	0.96	10.99	6.80	0.62	0.34	N = 1,456
Rich	33.74	31.30	39.43	31.30	45.93	N = 246
Total	2.56	7.44	5.20	2.29	3.14	N = 3,792

Chi square test value = 3.9478E-52; significant at p < 0.01

The profile of poverty in the deprivation of household possessions is almost the same in all the three panchayats. Most of the very poor have nothing – not even a radio or a bicycle. A considerable percentage of the rich possess almost all the luxury items.

Ownership of land

Table 5.45   Possession of land in the high-level panchayat (in %)

Extent of land (in cents)	Very poor	Poor	Middle-class	Rich	Total
0	12.70	3.64	1.44	0.41	3.51
1–5	55.70	16.96	1.44	0.41	13.87
6–10	24.35	19.66	1.51	0.00	11.89
11–50	6.99	40.20	10.10	3.25	22.86
51–100	0.26	15.26	10.51	4.06	11.18
Above 100	0.00	4.28	75	91.87	36.69
Total no. of families	N = 386	N = 1,704	N = 1,456	N = 246	N = 3,792

Key: 1 cent is 1% of an acre.
Chi square test value = 3.05768E-76; significant at $p < 0.01$

More families in the high-level panchayat, than in the other two panchayats are land-rich. The percentage of middle-class and rich households having more than 100 cents of land is the highest in the high-level panchayat.

Mean score for the three panchayats

It is clear from Table 5.46 that the high level panchayat ranks first in six out of the nine parameters in this study. It has the lowest scores in sanitation and occupation and ranks second in drinking water facility. It is also discernible from the table that land and possessions in the high-level panchayat contribute to the high rank.

Table 5.46   Mean score and relative rank of the panchayats

Items	Low-level panchayat		Mid-level panchayat		High-level panchayat	
	Mean score	Relative rank	Mean score	Relative rank	Mean score	Relative rank
Housing	3.39	3	3.68	2	**3.95**	1
Stove type	0.41	3	0.92	2	**1.02**	1
Cooking fuel	1.35	3	1.99	2	**2.32**	1
Drinking water	**1.07**	1	0.97	3	1.00	2
Sanitation	2.86	2	**3.22**	1	2.57	3
Occupation	1.98	2	**2.13**	1	1.79	3
Family mean size	−0.67	3	−0.63	2	**−0.61**	1
Possessions	7.43	3	8.67	2	**11.01**	1
Land	4.62	3	4.64	2	**14.38**	1
Overall mean score	22.45	3	25.60	2	**37.45**	1

A similar pattern is visible in the distribution of poverty/affluence. The highest percentage of very poor is in the low-level panchayat (23.87%) and they have the lowest score among the very poor of all three panchayats under study (5.78). Though the highest percentage of poor is in the mid-level panchayat (52.78%) the poor in the low-level panchayat have the least score. The highest percentage of middle-class (38.40%) and rich (6.49%) are in the high-level panchayat. Details of the poverty/affluence profile and the relative scores are given in Table 5.47.

Table 5.47   Economic stratification and mean scores

		Very poor	Poor	Middle -class	Rich	Total
Low-level panchayat	% of households	23.87	52.05	22.04	2.04	100.00
	Mean score	5.78	15.78	46.57	131.80	22.45
Mid-level panchayat	% of households	14.50	52.78	31.34	1.37	100.00
	Mean score	**6.89**	16.27	45.31	**133.88**	25.60
High-level panchayat	% of households	10.18	44.93	38.40	6.49	100.00
	Mean score	6.76	**16.58**	**53.99**	130.73	37.45

Section three: personal data analysis in the mid-level panchayat

As mentioned in section one, over and above the files on households, and facilities and possessions, an additional file, was made available with the following data on individual members of the family, in respect of the mid-level panchayat of Andoorkonam:

1.   Sex;
2.   Age;
3.   Marital status; and
4.   Education.

This enabled the analysis of the social and demographic characteristics of the household members in the mid-level panchayat. This panchayat has a population of 16,865 persons, with 8,201 males (48.63%) and 8,664 females (51.37%) and a sex ratio of 1,056 women for every 1,000 men.

Table 5.48 Age-wise composition and sex ratio* of population in the mid-level panchayat

Age-group	Male	Female	Sex ratio
60+	580	567	978
46–60	1,017	1,081	1,063
31–45	1,629	1,828	1,122
19–30	1,934	2,440	1,162
6–18	2,270	2,029	894
0–5	771	719	933

Key: * No. of females per every 1,000 men.

Figure 5.7 Composition of the population by age and sex in the mid-level panchayat

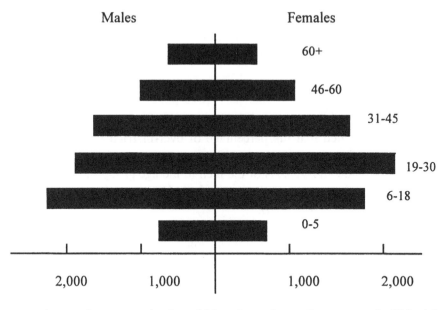

As per the survey, in the mid-level panchayat there are only 933 girls to 1,000 boys in the age group of 0–5. This is unusual.[10] The gender-wise total population in the age group of 0–4 provided in the National Censuses for the years 1961, 1971 and 1981, shows that in Kerala, for every 1,000

boys, there were 952, 965 and 969 girls respectively. In 1991 census, the data given is for children between the age group of 0–6, showing a sex ratio of 958 girls per every 1,000 boys.

The sex ratio of the elderly age group in the mid-level panchayat is also unfavourable to women. There are only 978 women per every 1,000 men. The census figures for this age group are not available. In general, the number of elderly women in Kerala is more than the number of elderly men. In the 60+ category, it is reported that there are 1,146 women to 1,000 men (Radhakrishnan, 1994). Since the reported life expectancy of females in Kerala is higher than men,[11] the unusually low number of females among the elderly in the mid-level panchayat is a puzzle.

Only a detailed investigation would reveal why the sex ratio among the younger and elderly age group is so unfavourable to women.

It is discernible from the survey data that till the age of 18, the sex ratio is unfavourable to women (904 women per every 1,000 men). The sex ratio among the age group of 19–45, is favourable to women (1,198 women per 1,000 men). Is it due to the high migration of men to other panchayats/cities/states/countries? This issue would be discussed in more detail while discussing marital status.

Gender and Marital Status

Ever-married persons

The survey revealed that the percentage of ever-married women is more than ever-married men in the mid-level panchayat of Andoorkonam. 65.98% of women and 51.20% of the men in the age group of 6 and above are ever-married (ever-married persons include those who are currently married, divorced, or widowed).

The percentage of ever-married persons in the 6–18 age group – 1.45% for men and 2.90% for women points to the fact that adolescent marriage[12] is still practised in Kerala. For want of information on the age at marriage, we cannot arrive at the percentage of persons who got married before the minimum legal age at marriage.[13]

Compared to men, women in Kerala get married at an earlier age. Against 73.40% of women, only 34.28% of men in the age group of 19–30 come under the ever-married category. This also means that a considerable percentage of women in this age group marry men aged above 30.

Table 5.49 **Composition of ever-married population in the mid-level panchayat**

Age-group	Ever-married men		Ever-married women	
	Number	Percentage[a]	Number	Percentage[b]
6–18	33	1.45	59	2.90
19–30	663	34.28	1,791	73.40
31–45	1,540	94.53	1,777	97.21
46–60	998	98.13	1,057	97.77
60 +	570	98.27	558	98.41
Above 6	3,804	51.20	5,242	65.98

Keys: [a] ever-married men as a percentage of the total male population in the respective age-groups; [b] ever-married women as a percentage of the total female population in the respective age-groups.

Marital status of men and women show a different picture in the age group of 30 plus. In the 31–45 age group, 94.53% of men and 97.21% of women are ever-married, in the 46–60 age-group, 98.13% of men and 97.77% of females are ever-married, and in 60+ age group, 98.27% men and 98.41% of women are ever-married.

Currently married persons

As a corollary to the above, it is found that currently married women out-number men (currently married persons exclude widows/widowers and the divorced). While 4,745 currently married women are living in the panchayat, only 3,719 married men live in the panchayat. In Kerala, as in the other parts of India, the majority of the married women stay either with their husbands' family, or set up nuclear families. Thus the absence of 1,026 married men may be a reflection of the migration of men for jobs abroad and to other parts of the state and other Indian states. This number may not be precise, when the number of married women who live away from their husbands and children because of their jobs is taken into consideration. However, in Kerala, more men than women leave homes for employment. So it is likely that more married men than married women are 'missing' from the data. Hence it can be safely assumed that a considerable percentage of 'missing men' in the currently married category are residing in other towns/states or abroad for occupational reasons. They have not been enumerated in the survey. For practical reasons, only persons who are permanently residing in a particular household are accounted for, in the national census also. This raises some fundamental questions about the belief that sex ratio in Kerala is favourable to women. How far has the out-migration of men from Kerala gone unaccounted for, in the census figures and in this survey? At best, we can identify the probable number of 'missing men' in the ever-married category in the mid-level panchayat. We cannot even 'guestimate' the number of unmarried men from the mid-level panchayat, residing outside the panchayat. They also might be 'missing' from the survey data. This leads to the question as to how far out-migration[14] of Malayali men has resulted in under-numeration of men in Kerala. Saradamoni (1994, 1995) raised this question. The *National Family Health Survey* 1992–93 comments that the extreme value[15] of sex ratio in Kerala is 'probably due to the selective out-migration of males from Kerala' (1995, p. 40).

Table 5.50   Composition of currently married population in the mid-level panchayat (in %)

Age-group	Currently married men		Currently married women	
	Number	Percentage[a]	Number	Percentage[b]
6–18	24	1.05	53	2.61
19–30	655	33.87	1,762	72.21
31–45	1,525	93.61	1,687	92.28
46–60	986	96.95	888	82.14
60 +	529	91.20	355	62.61
Above 6	3,719	50.05	4,745	59.72

Keys: [a] currently married men as a percentage of the total male population in the respective age-groups; [b] currently married women as a percentage of the total female population in the respective age-groups.

Two more points concerning the sex ratio in Kerala seem to be relevant here. The first one relates to the sex ratio among fisherfolk in Kerala. In 1993, The adult sex ratio among the marine fisherfolk population was 967 women per every 1,000 men and among the inland fisherfolk population, it was 965 women per every 1,000 men (*Women in Kerala*, 1994). It is true that the condition of fisherfolk women, when compared to the general population is not good. But the fisherfolk population seldom emigrate. So do the people of Wayanad and Idukki districts, where the sex ratio is unfavourable to women. As per the National Census 1991, there are 966 women per 1,000 men in Wayanad and 975 women per 1,000 men in Idukki. The Director of Census Operations, Kerala observes that this is 'apparently due to the hilly terrain and peculiar migration pattern' (1993, p. 7). It is not clear how the hilly terrain would affect natural demography. Moreover, if 'the peculiar migration pattern' means immigration of men into these districts, why is it that the Census Director is silent about the emigration of men from other districts? Only a detailed enquiry would reveal whether the sex ratios of Wayanad and Idukki are due to the absence of migration of men from these districts, or the presence of immigrant male population.

Widows and widowers

Table 5.51 shows the age-group wise percentage of widows and widowers among ever-married men and women in the mid-level panchayat.

Table 5.51   Widows and widowers in the mid-level panchayat (in %)

Age-group	Ever-married men (number)	Widowers (%)[a]	Ever-married women (number)	Widows (%)[b]
6–18	33	24.24[16]	59	6.77
19–30	663	0.75	1,791	0.28
31–45	1,540	1.29	1,777	3.43
46–60	998	1.00	1,057	5.71
60 +	570	6.14	558	36.02
Above 6	3,804	1.89	5,242	8.47

Keys: [a] widowers as a percentage of the ever-married male population in the respective age-groups; [b] widows as a percentage of the ever-married female population in the respective age-groups.

The percentage of widows is higher than the percentage of widowers. 444 women are widows and 72 men are widowers. Thus, widows constitute 8.47% of the ever-married women in the age group of 6+, while only 1.89% of the ever-married men in this age-group are widowers. The greater number of widows is likely to be due to a combination of factors:

1. High age gap among married couples, where the husband is older than wife;
2. More widowers than widows get remarried and
3. The death rates of men among all age groups, except, 10–14 are higher than those of women[17] (Sample Registration System 1991, cited in *Women in Kerala*, 1994).

The number of widows in the above 45 age-group (364) far exceeds the number of widowers (59) and the proportion of widows to widowers in this age-group is 6:1.

Divorce

Table 5.52 shows the age-group wise percentage of the divorced among ever-married men and women in the mid-level panchayat.

Table 5.52   Classification of divorce by gender in the mid-level panchayat

Age-group	Ever-married men (number)[a]	Divorced men[c] (%)	Ever-married women (number)[b]	Divorced women (%)[d]
6–18	25	4.00	55	3.64
19–30	658	0.45	1,776	0.78
31–45	1,526	0.06	1,716	1.68
46–60	988	0.20	894	0.44
60 +	535	1.12	357	0.56
Above 6	3,732	0.35	4,798	1.10

Keys: [a] excludes widowers; [b] excludes widows; [c] divorced men as a percentage of the ever-married male population in the respective age-groups; [d] divorced women as a percentage of the ever-married female population in the respective age-groups.

The number of divorced women who remain unmarried (53) exceeds the number of divorced men who remain unmarried (13). Thus, 0.35% of ever-married men (excluding widowers) are divorced and remain unmarried, while 1.10% of ever-married women (excluding widows) are divorced and remain unmarried.

Divorced women getting remarried is rare in Kerala. Divorced men more often get remarried. It can be discerned from the data there are four divorced women for every divorced male in the panchayat. Though the exact data is not available, it can be presumed that more divorced men than divorced women get remarried. Published data on divorce practices in Kerala society are not available. Informal communication with social workers reveals that usually men initiate the divorce proceedings. But during the course of proceedings, men often change their mind, but women insist on separation. Though the latest census figures on marital status are not readily available, the 1981 census shows that 0.29% of men and 1.40% of women among the ever-married category in Kerala, are either divorced or separated. The corresponding national figures are 0.10% men and 0.23% women, suggesting that at the national level too, it is also easier for men to re-marry.

Social class and marital status

The survey revealed that the percentage of ever-married women is more than ever-married men among all social classes of population in the mid-level panchayat of Andoorkonam. Among the scheduled caste population, 63.07% of women, (against 52.21% men) and among the scheduled tribes, 67.13% of women, (against 51.61% of men) are ever-married. The percentage of women and men ever-married among the general population is higher – 66.96% and 51.51% respectively.

Scheduled castes

Table 5.53   Composition of the ever-married population among scheduled castes in the mid-level panchayat

Age-group	Ever-married men[a]		Ever-married women[a]	
	Number	Percentage[b]	Number	Percentage[c]
6–18	11	2.88	13	3.84
19–30	128	39.62	264	67.00
31–45	264	92.95	288	92.60
46–60	143	96.62	150	93.75
60 +	68	95.77	64	98.46
Above 6	614	52.21	779	63.07

Keys: [a] includes currently married, divorced or widowed; [b] ever-married men as a percentage of the male population in the respective age-groups; [c] ever-married women as a percentage of the female population in the respective age-groups.

Scheduled tribes

Table 5.54   Composition of the ever-married population among scheduled tribes in the mid-level panchayat

Age-group	Ever-married men[a]		Ever-married women[a]	
	Number	Percentage[b]	Number	Percentage[c]
6–18	2	2.77	2	3.51
19–30	25	37.31	49	72.05
31–45	44	97.77	53	98.14
46–60	31	96.87	22	84.61
60 +	11	100	8	88.89
Above 6	113	49.78	134	63.81

Keys: [a] currently married, divorced or widowed; [b]ever-married men as a % of the male population in the respective age-groups; [c] ever-married women as a % of the female population in the respective age-groups.

General population

Table 5.55   Composition of the ever-married population among the general population in the mid-level panchayat

Age-group	Ever-married men[a]		Ever-married women[a]	
	Number	Percentage[b]	Number	Percentage[b]
6–18	20	1.12	43	2.68
19–30	506	33.22	1,454	74.41
31–45	1,211	94.75	1,407	97.91
46–60	813	98.54	879	98.87
60 +	483	98.77	479	98.55
Above 6	3,033	51.61	4,262	67.13

Key: [a] includes currently married, divorced or widowed; [b] ever-married men as a percentage of the male population in the respective age-groups; [c] ever-married women as a percentage of the female population in the respective age-groups.

Social class variations in marital status

Table 5.56 Social stratification and marital status in the mid-level panchayat

Age-group	Ever-married men (in %)[a]			Ever-married women (in %)[b]		
	SC	ST	General	SC	ST	General
6–18	2.88	2.77	1.12	3.84	3.51	2.68
19–30	39.62	37.31	33.22	67.00	72.05	74.41
31–45	92.95	97.77	94.75	92.60	94.44	97.91
46–60	96.62	96.87	98.54	93.75	84.61	98.87
60 +	95.77	100	98.77	98.46	88.89	98.55
Above 6	52.21	49.78	51.61	63.07	63.81	67.13

Keys: [a] ever-married men as a percentage of the male population in the respective age-groups; [b] ever-married women as a percentage of the female population in the respective age-groups.

The figures indicate that the percentage of ever-married persons below the age of 19 is higher for both men and women among scheduled castes and scheduled tribes. This indicates that persons getting married below the legally prescribed marriageable age are higher among the previously oppressed classes.

Social class variations in divorce

The rate and pattern of divorce among the three social classes differ. Among both men and women, the percentage of divorced among scheduled caste is more than the general population. One major reason could be the relatively lower percentage of re-marriage among both men and women belonging to scheduled castes. The data also shows that divorce is totally absent among the scheduled tribe community of this panchayat.

Table 5.57 Divorce rates among the various social classes in the mid-level panchayat (in %)

Social class	Scheduled caste		Scheduled tribe		General	
Gender	Men	Women	Men	Women	Men	Women
Percentage	1.09	2.46	0.00	0.00	0.27	0.65

Education

An analysis of the level of literacy and education shows that 92.96% of the population aged six and above, residing in the mid-level panchayat are literate. The majority (65.57%) of the population are classified as below SSLC (Secondary School Leaving Certificate), meaning they have not completed their secondary school leaving certificate course. These people have completed a few years of education at school. Some people in

Table 5.58   Level of literacy and education in the mid-level panchayat (in %)

Age	Sex	Level of literacy/education		
		Illiterates	SSLC	University
19-30	M	2.17	31.13	8.69
	F	3.20	28.87	10.98
31-45	M	5.22	19.34	8.16
	F	10.56	15.54	3.34
46-60	M	11.21	13.57	6.10
	F	21.46	7.12	1.48
60+	M	15.69	8.10	3.10
	F	33.51	1.76	0.71

Chi square test value = 3.5569E-286; significant at $p < 0.01$

this category might have dropped out of school, while some others might have failed in the SSLC examination. 18.19% of the population aged 5+ have passed the SSLC examination. 5.19% of the population aged 5+ have university education[18]. Table 5.58 shows that over the years, the educational qualifications of both males and females have increased considerably.

Social stratification and education

Table 5.59 reveals that the level of illiteracy is very high among elderly people in the scheduled castes and also among women of the general population. At the same time, it is also clear from this table that over the years, the level of illiteracy has been considerably reduced among all age groups irrespective of social class. The percentage of illiterates in the younger generation in all social classes, among both men and women, has dropped considerably.

Table 5.59 Social stratification and illiteracy in the mid-level panchayat (in %)

Age-group	Scheduled castes		Scheduled tribes		General	
	Male	Female	Male	Female	Male	Female
19–30	7.12	9.14	0.00	3.08	1.18	1.79
31–45	14.50	26.82	2.22	12.96	3.05	6.75
46–60	25.70	48.13	6.25	40.00	8.61	15.97
60+	40.80	49.23	9.09	22.22	11.50	31.48

Table 5.60 Social stratification and school education at the SSLC level in the mid-level panchayat (in %)

Age-group	Scheduled castes		Scheduled tribes		General	
	M	F	M	F	M	F
19–30	13.6	13.45	11.90	27.69	35.70	31.93
31–45	4.00	3.64	13.30	12.96	22.60	17.68
46–60	4.05	1.25	9.38	0.00	15.20	7.99
60+	1.41	1.54	9.09	11.11	8.79	1.65

Due to the improvement over the past few decades in the educational sector, the younger generation fares better than the older generation in completing school education. This applies to all the three social classes and for both men and women.

Table 5.61 shows that among the younger generation, there are more people with university education. The table also reveals that among the non-SC/ST population, more women in the younger age-group (19–30) have university education (8.13%) than men (6.63%). Among the scheduled tribe community, the percentage of women completing a high school degree in this age group is higher than men (Table 5.60). But the percentage of women in this age group with university education is lower than men (Table 5.61). It could be a reflection of the lower status ascribed to women among the schedule tribes. It is also discernible that the previously oppressed classes have not improved their academic achievements in comparison to the general population. At the same time, considering the rigid caste system in the past, it is not surprising that none of the scheduled castes and scheduled tribes above the age of 60 have any university degrees.

Table 5.61   Social stratification and university education in the mid-level panchayat (in %)

Age-group	Scheduled castes		Scheduled tribes		General	
	M	F	M	F	M	F
19–30	1.86	2.28	5.97	4.62	9.85	12.95
31–45	1.45	0.33	2.22	0.00	9.62	4.04
46–60	1.35	0.63	3.13	0.00	7.15	1.69
60+	0.00	0.00	0.00	0.00	3.68	0.82

Relationship between categories of sanitation and other variables

Sanitation is a basic human right. Lack of proper sanitation, therefore is a basic human deprivation. In order to understand the relationship between the various categories of sanitation and factors which influence the type of sanitation, Chi square tests of independence and coefficient of variation tests were conducted. Coefficient of variation is the ratio between standard deviation and mean value. Thus the coefficient of variation would help us analyze the variations between a given category of sanitation (open, without septic tank and septic tank) and the factors which influence those categories (social class, main source of income and levels of education of the head of households).

Social stratification

The coefficient of variation is high in the open space category. This means that the lower the social class, the lower is the type of toilet – in this case, lack of any sanitation facility. The low coefficient of variation in the second type of toilet leads to the conclusion that some households, irrespective of social class have toilets without septic tanks. In respect of toilets with septic tanks, though the coefficient of variation is not statistically significant, the high variance shows that social class influences the type of sanitation.

Table 5.62   Bi-variate relationship between sanitation and social class in the mid-level panchayat

Type of toilet	Scheduled castes	Scheduled tribes	General	Coefficient of variation
Open space	49.83	28.24	16.55	0.54
Without septic tank	25.00	27.06	29.31	0.08
With septic tank	25.17	44.70	54.14	0.36

Chi square test value = 2.6584E-65; significant at $p < 0.01$

Occupation

Table 5.63   Bi-variate relationship between sanitation and main source of income in the mid-level panchayat

	Type of sanitation		
Main source of income	Open	Without septic tank	With septic tank
Self-employment and others	9.76	44.02	46.22
Permanent job	13.45	28.43	58.12
Temporary job/coolie	31.34	26.92	41.74
Foreign remittance	20.00	17.50	62.50
Coefficient of variation	0.51	0.38	0.19

Chi square test value = 1.12E-45; significant at $p < 0.01$

The coefficient of variation is the highest in the open type. The variation among different levels of occupation and the lack of any sanitation is highly significant. Households with less secure and less income-generating employment are more likely to be deprived of toilet facilities.

Education

Table 5.64   Bi-variate relationship between sanitation and education in the mid-level panchayat

Type of toilet	Illiterates	Neo-literates	Below SSLC	SSLC and above[19]	Coefficient of variation
Open space	43.98	39.64	20.50	5.83	0.64
Without septic tank	27.39	31.36	32.45	15.67	0.29
With septic tank	28.63	28.99	47.05	76.49	0.51

Chi square test value = 1.986E-89; significant at $p < 0.01$

Education considerably influences the type of toilet available for the household members. Of all the variables tested, the coefficient of variation is highest in the absence of toilets (open space) for a particular level of education. The lower the level of education, the higher is the chance of using open spaces as toilets. Although level of education has the highest coefficient of variation among all three factors under study, it may be recalled that the variables are all inter-related. The more oppressed the social class, the lower their education; and the lower their level of employment. This is evident from the tables on levels of education and social class. Poverty is a vicious cycle, a trap.

Major findings

The visits to the panchayats revealed the harsh realities of life at the grass-roots level. There is a wide disparity between the rich and the poor in basic amenities like shelter and sanitation. The living conditions of the people in the 'One lakh housing' and 'Harijan' colonies are appalling. Unfortunately, these colonies have further marginalized the vulnerable and the oppressed sections from the mainstream society.

Despite the lack of basic amenities in schools, the teachers are not demoralized. They are very compassionate towards children. In all the panchayats, parents perceive education as a good investment for their children. At the same time, people like Ramakrishan Nair, find that education failed to provide their children with passports for a better life. The educated remain unemployed. But, despite the high unemployment, it is the workers from Tamil Nadu who lay telephone cables in these panchayats.

The poor quality of drinking water and the lack of toilet facilities were the most vital problems revealed during the visits to these panchayats. The sufferings of women, like the elderly widow in the low-level panchayat and the coir worker in the mid-level panchayat, deserve more attention and remedial action. It is high time that the government of Kerala shifts the focus from the macro indicators to the micro-realities.

The survey revealed that there is no uniform pattern of development in the three regions under study. The geographical division of low, mid and high land, matches generally to development indicators. Thus relatively low land is the least developed, mid-land, moderately developed and high land highly developed. This is obvious from the overall parameters described in section one and the mean scores of panchayats given in section two.

The Chi square tests of significance conducted to analyze the relationship between economic stratification (level of poverty/affluence) and the various variables (income, housing, sanitation, social stratification, drinking water, cooking fuel and stove, facilities and possessions) returned very high χ^2 values, showing significant association. The Chi square tests showed similar patterns of significant associations between economic stratification and the various variables in all the three panchayats. The survey also revealed that the overall living conditions of a considerable percentage of the population are far from satisfactory. The deprivation is quite significant in a basic amenity like sanitation. Only 69.13% of the entire households in these panchayats have some sort of man-made sanitation facility. Nearly 3,000 households and around 16,000 people of the three panchayats do not have any sanitation facility and this adversely affects the environment. The impact of these conditions on physical and emotional well-being of people, especially women, is severe. The Chi square tests conducted to analyze the relationship between sanitation and other variables revealed that social class, levels of income and education, have a significant impact on the quality of sanitation. The coefficient of variation tests also confirmed this finding. The more oppressed the class, lower their education, lower their level of income and hence higher the deprivation of this basic amenity. The previously oppressed classes have not so far escaped from the poverty trap, which denies them basic human dignity.

The housing situation in general is found to be unsatisfactory. Although the exact number of sub-standard houses in these panchayats is unknown, of the 3,547 kutcha houses, (mud and brickwork and thatched), at least 50% are either uninhabitable or dilapidated. It is also unacceptable that 91.92% i.e., 9,826 families are using crude stoves made from stones, either sides-open or sides-closed. This has a serious impact on the health conditions of the household members, especially women and children. The impact will be greater for poor people, whose huts being tiny and the density of population where they live, are quite high. What this data has not revealed is the quality of drinking water the poor in these panchayats have. There again, the visits to the panchayats revealed that due to the unsanitary conditions, the wells are polluted.

The disparity between the rich and the poorer sections of the panchayats is very wide. In land, facilities and possessions, the gap between these classes is quite prominent. It may be noted that this survey has not attempted to find out the savings of the population, in terms of currency or gold. When we imagine what the rich have and what the poor do not have, the disparity is much more than what is reflected in the survey. Four decades after the formation of the state, it is shameful that 35.52% of the households in these panchayats do not even have electricity in their homes.

Despite the efforts of the government to improve the condition of the previously oppressed classes, the majority of the scheduled castes and scheduled tribes remain poor, as revealed by the social stratification tables in section two (Table 5.19). Though these people have definitely improved their educational level over the years, there is a wide gap between the previously oppressed classes and the general population.

On the brighter side, the educational qualifications of the younger generation have improved considerably. Young women have better educational qualifications. On the other hand, household industry, which would provide employment especially to women, is virtually absent in all the panchayats.

The results of the survey raise some fundamental questions about the sex ratio in Kerala, supposed to be favourable to women. Only a detailed investigation into this aspect, taking the number of male emigrants (and female emigrants, through they are relatively smaller in number) into account will give a true picture of the sex ratio in Kerala.

The social fabric is weakening in Kerala. Divorce is on the increase, which, in many instances, could be better for the women concerned. Also of concern is the low percentage of divorced women who re-marry. As the data show, it is much easier for divorced men to re-marry. In respect of widowhood also, the number of widows in all ages is more than the number of widowers[20] and here again, it is possible that widowers get remarried, while widows remain unmarried. The quality of life of divorced or abandoned women, especially the elderly, is generally not good. Even those widows, who are lucky enough to receive a widow pension, have to struggle hard to make both ends meet with the meagre amount of the pension, Rs. 100 per month. Nuclear families have almost become a norm of the Kerala society and at least in several cases, the elderly widows are left uncared for, or at the mercy of organized sectors for care.

On the basis of what has been discussed so far, the next chapter would summarize the illusions and realities of social development in Kerala.

Notes

1   Unless specified, 'levels' refer to geographical levels, and not, to the levels of development.
2   Several organizations, including The Kerala State Land Use Board (KSLUB); the Integrated Rural Technology Centre (IRTC); Kerala Sasthra Sahithya Parishad (KSSP); Department of Science and Technology, New Delhi; Science, Technology and Environment Committee, Kerala; and State Planning Board, Trivandrum, contributed to the resource mapping programme.
3   However, to an extent, the marginalization of fisherfolk and tribals has been dealt with in Chapter 4.
4   To hasten the 'qureying' process, one way around would have been to bring the personal data on to Excel spreadsheets. But as the data set had 16,865 rows which is more than the maximum row limit in Excel (16,384), I had to continue working on dBASE IV.

5   The Chi square test for independence returns the values from the Chi-squared (χ^2) distributions for the statistic and the appropriate degrees of freedom. This test is a measure to see the extent to which the observed frequencies differ from the expected frequencies, *if there had been no association*. If the *observed differs sufficiently from the expected*, we can say there is an association.

6   A reflection of the paradox of labour scarcity despite severe macro unemployment, as discussed in Chapter 2.

7   *Congee*, or *kanji*, the traditional rice porridge.

8   vernacular cigarettes.

9   One lakh is 0.1 million.

10   Is it possible that this could be the result of sex-selective abortion/female infanticide/female malnutrition? However, there is no supporting evidence in the Kerala context. Sex-selective abortion, female infanticide and female malnutrition have not so far caught any media attention. In Kerala, the media is vigilant and would never hesitate to take up similar social issues, or build up campaigns. Only a detailed investigation would give insights into the reasons for the sex ratio among this age group being so skewed against females.

11   According to *Economic Review*, 1995, in the year 1991–92, the female life expectancy was 72.5, against the male life expectancy of 69.

12   Marriage in the period between being a child and being a grown person.

13   According to the Child Marriage Restraint Act of 1978, the minimum legal age at marriage in India, is 18 years for women; and 21 years for men.

14   There is no secondary data source which would provide satisfactory information on the number of Keralites working abroad and in other Indian states.

15   In their survey, the sex ratio in Kerala was found to be 1,068 females per 1,000 males; higher than the census figure of 1,036 females per 1,000 males.

16   8 men below the age of 18 – i.e. 24.24% of the ever-married men in this age-group are widowers. This seems puzzling.

17   This is a universal phenomenon when women are given equal access to survival sources.

18   Includes diploma holders, graduates and post-graduates.

19   Since the frequency under the category, 'open space' and university education was below the required number to do Chi-square evaluation, the categories of SSLC and university education have been combined.

20   the only exception is the age group of 6–18 – against 4 widows, there are 8 widowers.

6   Realities and Illusions of Social Development in Kerala

It is a reality that ...

People in Kerala do live longer than in other parts of India. Few infants and children die in Kerala; more women are admitted to hospitals for delivery; maternal mortality and fertility rates are low; there are no reported cases of female infanticides and no sexual discrimination on the part of government in the provision of health care and education. The mean age at marriage for both men and women in Kerala is higher than the all-India average.

In Kerala, people have access to schools, health care systems and communication facilities and they do utilize these facilities. Women and men in Kerala have achieved a level of literacy higher than that in any other Indian state. The public distribution system is near-universal, without an urban bias as in the other Indian states.

The previously oppressed castes, who were denied social participation in the past, do participate now in all walks of society. A region which had once practised the most cruel and rigid caste system in India, which banned lower castes from public markets and which made low caste women go naked above the waist, today, is the least caste conscious region of India.

Kerala has achieved higher scores in Physical Quality of Life Index than would be expected based on its State Domestic Product. The Kerala state government has been spending a substantial amount on social sectors, an amount significantly higher than what could be expected based on its SDP. The state government has introduced several social welfare and security measures and has been successful to a great extent in bridging the inter-regional gaps.

Historical and geographical factors have been conducive to social development in Kerala. Interactions with foreigners in trade and commerce and the presence of benevolent Maharajas, Christian missionaries, a strong communist movement – all these helped Kerala achieve higher PQLI. The fertile land and the availability of water helped an even settlement pattern, which in turn has prevented the spreading of communicable diseases. The high density of population facilitated the delivery of, and access to, health care and education.

At the same time, macro-realities hide several unpleasant micro-realities. The texture of the quality of life at the grass roots level is not fully revealed by the rather impressive macro-indicators. The quantitative nature of social indicators has inherent limitations in assessing the qualitative aspects of the realities at the grass-roots level. At best, these indicators can assess the inter-regional differences in a country, but inherently fail to assess the intra-regional disparities. The inter-caste/class disparities in development disappear in the over-all development scenario. The state of marginalized groups like tribals or fisherfolk, living below the power, pollution and poverty lines is not reflected in the regional indicators.

People live longer, but ...

Martin (1979) wrote that a 'longer life need not be a better one'. Does the Kerala experience endorse this view? The high morbidity and low mortality paradox has been examined by previous studies (Panikar and Soman, 1984; Kannan et. al, 1991). Since comparable data for other states is not readily available, Kerala cannot be put in its perspective. But, the prevalence rate[1] of communicable diseases in Kerala does not give a healthy picture (*Economic Review*, 1995). While the rates for leprosy (0.22/1,000) and tuberculosis (1.26/1,000) may seem moderate, the rates for acute diarrhoea (199.86/1,000) and acute respiratory infection including pneumonia (770.12/1,000) are alarmingly high..

In a message by the Director General of the WHO (1995), he observed that for millions of people all over the world, 'for whom survival is a daily battle, the prospect of a longer life may seem more like a punishment than a prize'. Insecurity and uncertainty about food, clothing, shelter and health care, at any age can never be pleasant. The elderly feels the insecurity and uncertainty of the 'disease of poverty' more intensely.

Living in dilapidated huts, with no one to take care of them, suffering from arthritis and rheumatism, deafness and poor vision, walking all alone late at night in search of a corner to attend to nature's calls – are all dehumanizing experiences. No amount of statistics and none of the indicators would reflect the pathos and degradation of the frail elderly living in such deprived conditions. They are not numbers, they are human beings. For them, living longer means more years of sickness and deprivation. The frail elderly in the three panchayats are 'living examples' of this sad deprivation in Kerala society.

Women live longer, but ...

The hospitalization records furnished by the government of Kerala (*Women in Kerala*, 1994) show that the number of women undergoing treatment in Kerala is more than the number of men. For example, in 1991, 652,425 women (as against 485,930 men) registered as outpatients and 11,864,891 women, (as against 7,932,196 men) registered as inpatients in government allopathic institutions of Kerala.[2] This does not include people treated in the private hospitals and clinics or in the ayurvedic and homeopathic institutions of the government. The KSSP study (Kannan et. al, 1991) showed that in Kerala, the prevalence of acute morbidity and chronic diseases are higher among women than in men.

Like any other patriarchal society, a woman's workload in Kerala is much higher than that of a man – she does the shopping, she waits for a litre of palm oil in a never-ending queue, she bears all the burden of cooking, cleaning, washing and she takes care of the children and looks after the elderly parents of her husband (and more rarely her own parents). Even then, men in Kerala are prone to say about their respective wives that 'she is doing nothing' (*Aval onnum cheyyunnilla*).

Even the burden of 'planning the family' rests on the women in Kerala. Though male sterilization is an easier, simpler and more cost-effective method of family planning, in Kerala it is the women and not men who undergo sterilization. For example, 131,173 women, underwent sterilization in 1993, against 735 men (Suresh Babu, 1995). Over the years, the number of male sterilizations has dropped considerably.[3]

The high percentage of divorced and widowed women in the macro-level State data and the micro-level panchayat data reflects the status of women in Kerala society. More women than men remain unmarried after being divorced and widowed. A considerable percentage of the women, currently married, have to shoulder the responsibility of looking after the family when their men are away in pursuit of jobs. For the widows, life is not easy and even those who have pensions cannot survive decently with the meagre monthly pension of Rs. 100.

Children attend schools, but ...

Are they getting proper education? The illiteracy level among primary school children is very high. Though the drop-out rates among school going children is quite low,[4] 50% of the children appearing for the school final examination fail in the examination.[5] On the one hand, the low pass percentage, despite 'moderation' is a sad reflection of the quality of education in Kerala. On the other hand, for those students who fail in the Secondary School Leaving Certificate examination, there are neither vocational training courses nor opportunities to learn skills that might be useful to the present day world.

People are educated, but ...

Unfortunately, people in Kerala are 'educated to be unemployed'. Unemployment not only affects the individual's economic capability, but also his or her domestic and social life capabilities. It cripples the soul, and makes one feel unwanted and useless. The chronic unemployment and under-employment situation has forced men in Kerala to emigrate in search of jobs, leaving their families behind. This has adversely affected the social fabric of Kerala. This out-migration has left elderly persons, either uncared for, or at the mercy of old-age homes. The unemployment has also contributed to an increase in the number of suicides among youth in Kerala.[6] One may even speculate how far the unemployment situation has contributed to the higher mean age of marriage in the Kerala society.

Chronic unemployment, but ...

Streeten's (1981) observation that a large part of unemployment in Sri Lanka is the result of the high aims of the educated, who are no longer prepared to accept 'dirty' manual jobs, holds good for Kerala also. As in several other societies, a manual job is held in contempt in Kerala. Thus, despite high levels of unemployment, there is a heavy influx of workers from the neighbouring state of Tamil Nadu for doing manual labour. National Forum (*Deseeyavedi*) even goes to the extent of calling Kerala a 'mini-gulf' for the Tamil workers (1995). Workers from Tamil Nadu can be seen everywhere in Kerala engaged in manual work.[7]

Women are educated, but ...

Education has heightened the aspirations of women in Kerala. But lack of economic development has prevented them from entering the labour market. Census figures reveal that the female work participation rate is much lower than in the other Indian states, and over the years, female work participation is getting lower. In several sectors, there still is discrimination at work. For example, during the year 1993–94, the daily wages for women construction workers in the rural sector was Rs. 40.89 against Rs. 50.36 for men; in the urban sector, it was Rs. 42.80 for women, against Rs. 52.85 for men. In the agricultural sector, the wages were Rs. 32.31 for women and Rs. 48.40 for men, in 1993 (*Economic Review*, 1995).

Government is omnipresent, but ...

The state government intervenes in economic, social and even the cultural aspects of Kerala. In the economic sector, 48 out of 59 public sector enterprises have accumulated losses amounting to Rs. 6,732.80 million against their paid up capital of Rs. 5,408.60 million. In the social sector, the government took over and institutionalized a very strong people's library movement, and bureaucratized the people's literacy movement,[8] thereby 'killing people's initiatives' (interview with Kannan). The government politicized the co-operative movement, and even formed an organization for the promotion of eco-architecture defying the basic principles of the eco-sensitive and cost-effective architectural movement started by Dr. Laurie Baker.

The state of the health sector in Kerala shows that the government has failed to ensure quality of health care services. Studies by KSSP (1991), NSS surveys (cited in Sadanandan, 1993) and Kunhikannan and Aravindan (1994) show that even poor people in Kerala prefer private hospitals to government hospitals. This reflects the quality of services in the government health sector. An interview with Anand, the senior health official in Kerala, reflects the inherent contradictions in the government health policy. The official complained about the preference given to medical colleges at the cost of primary health centres, while on the other hand, advocated starting up new medical colleges in the joint/private sector. Starting new medical educational institutions providing specialized medical care, when basic medical facilities are not being provided at the rural health centres, is to say the least, a lop-sided priority.

Public toilets, 'maintained' by government are a reflection of the quality of services in Kerala. Baker (1995), has commented on the 'public conveniences' in Kerala:

> Seven out of ten users do NOT flush pans adequately. Four out of ten flush-tanks either do not work, or have no water in them or the handle or the knob is missing. Visit almost any public convenience (e.g., such as those outside the Medical College Hospital in Trivandrum) and you hurriedly turn away and leave in disgust (p. 16).

The previously oppressed classes have improved their position, but ...

Government of Kerala admits that despite efforts to improve the living conditions of the scheduled castes and scheduled tribes, the majority of the colonies in which the scheduled caste and scheduled tribe population live do not have basic amenities. There are scheduled caste/tribe colonies without proper housing, drinking water, electricity and transport (SC/ST devt. spl. cell dept. no. 43/91 dated 12 November 1991). Our analysis of panchayat data also show that the majority of the scheduled castes and scheduled tribe families live in absolute poverty and though the younger generation has improved their educational attainment, their achievements are lower than that of the general population.

Social scientists and development experience in Kerala

Development writers, who do not have a first hand experience of Kerala society tend to over-state the successes of Kerala society. For example, Elson (1994) wrote:

> An important aspect of this success lies in systems of accountability, which went far beyond occasional voting in parliamentary elections, and ensured that public expenditure was effective. Officials were held accountable not just for making adequate budgetary allocations to health and education expenditure, but also for ensuring health and education services as planned (p. 77).

One would wish it were true.

Even an anthropologist like Mencher, with a high level of exposure to Indian realities writes:

> ... in Kerala, if a PHC (Public Health Centre) was unmanned for a few days, there would be massive demonstration at the nearest collectorate (regional government office) led by local leftists, who would demand to be given what they knew they were entitled to (cited in Franke and Chasin, 1994, p. 45).

The health officials themselves admit that vacancies in primary health centres of 'backward districts' like Wayanad, Kasargod and Palghat remain unfilled 'because doctors refuse to work there' (interview with Appu). Even where doctors are posted, there are no medicines (interview with Anand). Several people in the panchayats under study complained about the lack of facilities and medicines in primary health centres. Above all, there is corruption and the unholy nexus between doctors, pharmaceutical companies and private laboratories, with the result that the doctors over-prescribe medicines, and suggest unnecessary and expensive laboratory tests (interview with Appu).

McKibben (1995), with all good intentions of being a strong believer in sustainable development, writes on Kerala:

> Kerala suggests a way out of two problems simultaneously: not only the classic development goal of more calories in bellies and more shoes on feet, but also the emerging equally essential, task of living *lightly* on the earth, using fewer resources, creating less waste (p.163).

Like anywhere else, the rich in Kerala live 'heavily' on the earth, except for their low fertility rates.[9] Those people who live lightly on the earth, 'sleeping on the floor', without many possessions, do so, not out of ecological consciousness, as one would like to believe, but because they cannot afford even the essential possessions. Kerala has not been successful in solving the problems of hunger for many of its people Even today, not everyone in Kerala can afford a pair of 'chappals', leave alone shoes!

Conclusion

Going by the strictest parameters of PQLI, we could safely conclude that Kerala has achieved social development. The term 'Model' literally means that which can act as a perfect example of something, for others to copy (*Longman Active Study Dictionary of English*, 1991). Can Kerala's development be called a model of development? Development is an all-encompassing term, which includes both economic and social aspects. Since the state is lagging behind several other Indian states in economic development, it is doubtful whether Kerala's development path can be called a model. As UNICEF (1996) rightly points out, economic and social development have to go hand in hand, otherwise one would pull the other down. In that sense, the apprehensions of P.K.V. Nair (1995), mentioned previously,[10] are valid. The economic crisis that Kerala is facing and the budget crunch as well as financial black-outs in the form of stopping government payments may lead us to question the sustainability of the model. The salient question here is how Kerala can 'survive' in its social development pursuits, considering the financial deficits and the global liberalization efforts where the state is withdrawing and markets are taking over. Theoretically, adjustments could be with a human face, but not necessarily so in practice. In a fragile federal system of fund transfers, allotments and plan budgeting, the social sector might get a smaller share and it would affect a state like Kerala more than it would affect any other

Indian state. At the same time, it is possible as the literature shows (for example, Newman and Thomson, 1989) that social development might lead to Kerala's economic development. With the right entrepreneurial climate and attitude, it might be possible that Kerala may in future be successful in utilizing its strong human resource base for economic development (Heller, 1995).

What went wrong on the economic front? Have the highly interventionist policies of the state government been detrimental to economic development? Neo-liberalists would argue that the government policies were mistaken both in conceptualisation and implementation. Rimmer (1984) argues that the driving force behind government policies is political, rather than economic, and is for sustaining power. The neo-liberal economists' argument that the state and the market are incompatible mechanisms for the pursuit of social development goals, is now being increasingly questioned (MacPherson, 1995). Lipton (1995) argues that the redistributive reforms in Asia proved disappointing for want of market reforms. 'Pure' market reforms in many developing countries since 1980, also proved disappointing, because the decline in redistributive reforms left many poor people without access to markets, land, or education. MacPherson's (1995) observation that the World Bank recently has focussed more on human resource development, holds good for World Bank studies on India also. For example, *Country Economic Memorandum on India* (World Bank, 1995) highlights the benefits of primary education and 'prescribes' more governmental intervention and investment.

Is the 'market' a solution to Kerala's economic problems? It is an extremely difficult question to answer. On the one hand, there is truth in R. Gandhi's (1993) observation that while the 'IMF and World Bank speak of integrating us into the world economy', 'the vast majority of Indians are not even integrated into the Indian economy' (cited in Seabrook, p. 233). On the other hand, it is also true that the state sector in Kerala has not been successful. But again, as R. Gandhi (1993) argues, 'the private sector in India is no paragon of virtue, whether in terms of paying its taxes, observing pollution laws, research and development or long-term planning'. It would be naive to believe that the world systems and multi-national corporations would be interested in the 'welfare of the people'. As V. George (1988) observes, the third world countries cannot avoid intervening on a large scale when they are faced with such national issues as deforestation, desertification and the like. At the same time, there need to be debates on the extent and form of government interventions.

These should not be construed as something to belittle Kerala's achievements, which are impressive from a national angle. Again since 'trickling-up' occurs more than 'trickling-down', by no means can it be said that the Kerala development experience has gone astray. Dubbing the Kerala experience as anti-growth does not make the discussion more profound. Naturally, investment in human resources and prioritization of social sectors have yielded results to a considerable extent as revealed by the simple indicators of literacy, life expectancy and infant mortality. On the other hand, there is no measuring device by which we can put the time machine in reverse and say 'had there been more emphasis on economic development'. It cannot be argued with certainty that Kerala might have succeeded in achieving economic growth; and more important, there is no assurance that economic development, if at all attained, might have led to the existing PQLI. Had economic growth automatically ensured human development or human welfare, then the social development aspects of several middle-east countries might have been far better.

Thus if life expectancy, literacy and infant mortality are sure indicators of social development, we can very well say that Kerala is a model of social development. This itself takes into account the fact that Kerala has utilized its economic resources to cater to social needs. In that sense and in that sense alone, the Kerala model of development exists. As Franke and Chasin (1991) point out, the Kerala development experience proves that one need not wait for economic development to invest in improving physical qualities of life.

Does this imply that Kerala development is exclusively the result of the good deeds of benevolent leaders – past and present? In reality, before and after the formation of Kerala state, the rulers and the ruling parties were responding to public demand, be it explicitly aired or not. Perhaps, that is precisely why there is no difference in the election manifestos of different parties – left, right or centrist. These manifest the people's aspirations for an egalitarian society and they do expect significant governmental interventions. When Kerala made history[11] by electing a communist government in 1957, people were seeking something – something better. Even now, when Kerala goes on alternating the ruling elite in every election, are the Keralites, despite their high party loyalty (Eldersveld, 1973) putting politicians and political parties in their place?

At the same time, as this study proves, all is not well in *God's own country*.[12] While the intentions of the social development pursuits in Kerala has been laudable, it has failed in ensuring a minimum quality of life for its people. With the implementation of 'structural adjustments', liberalization and privatisation, the state would be redefining its role.[13] Studies at national level have shown that the liberalization programmes have so far been detrimental to the interests of the rural poor.[14] The economic constraints that the state of Kerala faces will make it more difficult to pursue social aspects of development, once the central government gives less priority to social sectors. Withdrawal (even partial) of the state from the social sectors will adversely affect a considerable percentage of the population in Kerala. *World Development Report 1996* reports that in several countries, women have been adversely affected[15] in the transition from 'plan to market' – child care facilities have dramatically declined, health care systems have deteriorated and most often, women are laid off before men and women account for 'a disproportionate share of the unemployed' (p. 72).

Plan, or market, or a combination of both, the model that is proposed in this research is relevant because Kerala cannot sustain or improve the quality of life of its people without economic development. The model, adopting the Chinese concept of *yin* and *yang*, emphasized the harmony between economic and social aspects of development (p. 7). The disharmony in Kerala's development experience is the lack of economic development. The social inputs of health, education and other basic needs require economic inputs. Without a fair amount of growth, social development pursuits are unsustainable. The socio-economic dimensions of development are highly interactive and complementary. The dilemmas that Kerala society face now are due to the lack of economic growth. Attempts to sustain social development, without supportive economic development will be at the cost of quality and are not sustainable. As K.K. George (1994) observes, 'only higher incomes of households would enable them to obtain better nutrition, medical care and education Only economic growth can sustain, in the long run a state's capacity to provide public services, though growth by itself may not ensure it' (p. 15). Kerala's development experience proves that economic development, though it may not be a sufficient condition, is a necessary condition for social development. Seers (1977) identified poverty, unemployment and inequality as measures of development. The macro-level data proves that unemployment is very high in Kerala and the micro-level analysis shows that there is a high incidence of poverty in Kerala, as is reflected in the quality of housing, sanitation, cooking methods and fuel, facilities and possessions. Kerala needs economic growth and policies for employment generation. At the same time, economic growth alone will not result in social development. There are no simple solutions and the creative socio-economic policy directions that Kerala opts for now, will decide the course of Kerala's development path.

This research shows that the picture of macro-level realities hides several harsh micro-realities. The inherent limitation of the macro-level social indicators is that they are incapable of revealing the inter-regional and inter-class disparities in development. This research also shows that those sections of people, who were previously oppressed, still remain comparatively oppressed. The level of literacy and possessions among the scheduled castes and scheduled tribes point in this direction. What is surprising is that while most of the officials interviewed were conscious of the poor living conditions and physical quality of life of the scheduled tribes, the equally sad state of scheduled castes does not seem too apparent in development discussions among academics and in government circles.

Contrary to Kerala's image, the bureaucracy has adopted a top-down approach in development. Both the government and political parties seem to be following the same approach. On the one hand, few officials seek participation and on the other hand, people generally delegate authority to leaders of political parties.

Too much dependency on government in development pursuits has negative impacts. The literacy mission of 1991 is a case in point. Within four years from being a 'totally literate' state, the majority of neo-literates have gone back to the state of illiteracy. This is due to the high politicalization of Kerala society, wherein each new coalition ministry abandons schemes introduced by the previous ministry, run by its political rivals. The tragedy of the Kerala literacy mission was that KSSP, the non-governmental organization actively involved in the literacy mission, also backed out when the new government withdrew its support of the literacy mission. Ideally, KSSP, with its mass base of activists should have pursued the mission further, irrespective of governmental involvement.

Kerala development experience raises some basic questions. What is development without access to safe drinking water, toilets that would ensure privacy and hygiene, employment that would provide the means to make both ends meet? 'Total literacy' and all other educational achievements can not substitute for the essential requirements for living with dignity. Any society that is insensitive and indifferent to the primary needs of the people does not deserve to be called socially developed, much less a 'model' for the rest of the world.

Notes

1   calculated per 1,000 population exposed to risk.

2   The available literature on health utilization do not deal with the gender differences in utilization of government/private health care systems. An exception is the study conducted by Ramankutty, Vijayakumar and Soman (1992), *The pattern of morbidity in pre-school children in Rural Kerala*, cited by Ramankutty (1993), which found no gender difference in health care utilization. Only a detailed study of health care utilization in Kerala would shed light on the reason why more women than men utilize government health care facilities.

3   From 1957 to 1973, the number of male sterilizations were much higher than female sterilizations (for example, during the years, 1957–66, 88,855 men and 26,307 women underwent sterilization). By 1977, a reversal process took place. In 1977, only 15,285 men against 67,524 women got sterilized. By 1984, against a six digit number of females, a five digit number of males underwent the operation. In the late 1980s, the number of men sterilization was in four digits, against a six digit number of women sterilization (Kurup, 1991).

4   this by itself is no mean achievement, considering the fact that the school enrolment rate in Kerala is much higher than in any other Indian state.

5   students getting 35% marks in the examination are declared passed and every year, 'moderation' (giving a specific number of 'free' marks to increase the percentage of pass) is given to students who have failed.

6   KSSP (1987) found that the rate of suicide among the 20–24 age-group is 80.7/100,000, the highest among all age groups.

7   A study by *Deseeyavedi* (1995) found that 15.91% of the agricultural labourers in Kerala are workers from Tamil Nadu and 62.5% of the construction workers in Kerala are Tamilians.

8   Krishnakumar (1994) has written on the library movement in Kerala. Kerala has had a unique tradition of community libraries. This was the result of a library movement, based on popular participation. *Kerala Granthasala Sangham* (KGS) was formally registered in 1947 and by 1958, as Kusum Nair wrote: almost every village has a

genuine library with anything from 1,000 to 4,000 books and several hundred members. Member libraries received a grant-in-aid from the KGS. In 1977, the state government took over KGS through an ordinance. Library movement became a bureaucratic exercise, lost its soul and community support. Now the libraries in Kerala are in a sad state of affairs. There are few books and whatever is available is left unclassified. The buildings and furniture need maintenance. Reflecting a sad state of neglect and indifference, the library movement in Kerala is breathing its last.

Radhakrishnan (1996) reports from Kerala that for want of follow-up action, the literacy mission has failed in Kerala. A majority (75%) of the neo-literates in Kerala have gone back to the state of illiteracy. The post-literacy campaign of continuing education miserably collapsed in Kerala, with the result that the neo-literates relapsed into illiteracy.

9   Mahesh (1994) observes that household consumption in Kerala has increased tremendously, during the last two decades, and the disparity in consumption between the rich and the poor has thrown up various social and political problems.

10   Please see Chapter 3.

11   Apart from the tiny Italian principality of San Marino, it was the first case of a democratically elected communist government in the world (Nossiter, 1982).

12   This is how the Kerala Tourism Development Department promotes Kerala.

13   World Bank (1995) reports that the following reforms have been initiated in Kerala: closure and reorganization of public enterprises; zero-based budgeting or other mechanisms for expenditure programme review; compressing operating costs without neglecting vital expenditure such as maintenance and medical supplies.

     As a measure of liberalization, some public services, till now undertaken by the government, like mosquito control, garbage collection and disposal and street cleaning, maintenance of bus terminus/shelter in the city of Cochin, etc. have been given on a contract basis to the private sector.

14   Dev (1995) argues that the decline in rural non-agricultural employment and income; decline in fertiliser subsidies; reduction in central expenditure on anti-poverty programmes; and decline in expenditures on sectors which improve social consumption could be directly attributed to the reforms and increase in the issue prices of PDS, indirectly to reforms.

15   In repect of life expectancy, in Russia, male life expectancy fell by six years between 1990 and 1994 (from sixty-four to fifty-eight) and that of women by three years, from seventy-four to seventy-one. In Hungary, 'the poor regions and those going through the greatest socio-economic shock are starting to see mortality rates rise' (p. 128).

Bibliography

Acharya, P. (1995), 'Problems of Universal Elementary Education', *Economic and Political Weekly*, 3 December 1994.

Agnihotri, S.B. (1995), 'Missing Females: A Disaggregated Analysis', *Economic and Political Weekly*, 19 August 1995.

Alexander, K.C. (1974), 'Land Reforms in Kerala since Independence', *Behavioural Sciences and Community Development*, September 1974.

Alvis, M.H.M. (1991), 'Four Comments on Kerala', *Monthly Review*, January 1991.

Amin, S. (1991), 'Four Comments on Kerala', *Monthly Review*, January 1991.

Antia, N. H. (1997), 'Public health for private gain: proposal for new institute', *Economic and Political Weekly*, 32(32), 2019-20.

Antony, A.K. (1995), 'Kerala Model neglected productive aspects, says A.K. Antony', *The Hindu*, 25 September 1995.

Asia Times, 'India starting to miss its women', 21 June 1996, New Delhi.

Baby, A. A. (1996), 'Trends in Agricultural Wages in Kerala', Centre for Development Studies, Thiruvananthapuram, Occasional Paper Series.

Baker, L.W. (1995), 'Sabarimala: A study to see what can be done about some of the problems that inevitably arise when lakhs of people all want to go to the same place at one brief season each year', Unpublished report submitted to the Government of Kerala.

Balachandran, E. (1998), 'Kerala: learning the strengths of regionalism', *Economic and Political Weekly*, 33(9): 453.

Bandyopadhyay, D. (1997), 'People's participation in planning: Kerala experiment', *Economic and Political Weekly*, 32(39): 2450-54.

British Broadcasting Corporation (1992), 'Lessons from Kerala' (video recording), A production for the Open University, BBC.

Caldwell, C.J. (1986), 'Routes to Low Mortality in Poor Countries', *Population and Development Review*, June, 1986.

Caldwell, J.C. (1986), 'Routes to Low Mortality in Poor Countries', *Population and Demographic Review*, June, 1986.

Canadian Broadcasting Corporation (1988), 'Women of Kerala' (videorecording).

Centre for Monitoring Indian Economy (1994), *Basic Statistics: States*, New Delhi.

CESS (1991), *Panchayat Level Resource Mapping: An Approach Paper* – A Model for Micro Level Resource Survey with People's Participation, Trivandrum.

Chandran, K.N. (1994), 'Literacy in India and the Example of Kerala', *Journal of Reading*, March, 1994.

Dallago, B. (1991), 'Convergence, evolution and disruption of economic systems', Dallago, B., Brezinski, H. and Andreff, W. (eds), *Convergence and System Change*, Dartmouth, Aldershot.

David, J. (1990), *Levels of Socio-economic Development Theory*, Praeger, New York.

David, L.A. and Wilford, T.W. (1979), 'The Physical Quality of Life Index: A Useful Social Indicator?' in *World Development*, Vol. 7, 1979.

Deseeyavedhi (National Forum) (1995), 'Kerala, 'Mini-Gulf' of the Tamilians', Press release, 6 August 1995.

Dev, S.M. (1995), 'Economic Reforms and the Rural Poor', *Economic and Political Weekly*, 19 August 1995.

Dreze, J. and Loh, J. (1995), 'Literacy in India and China', *Economic and Political Weekly*, 11 November 1995.

Eapen, M. (1994), 'Employment and Unemployment in Kerala – An Analysis of Recent Trends', paper presented at the International Congress on Kerala Studies, 27–29 August, 1994, Thiruvananthapuram.

Eapen, M. (1994), 'Rural Non-Agricultural Employment in Kerala: Some Emerging Tendencies', *Economic and Political Weekly*, 21 May 1994.

Eldersveld, J.S., (1973), 'Party Identification in India in Comparative Perspective', *Comparative Political Studies*, Vol. 6, No. 3, October 1973.

Elson, D. (1994), 'Transition to the Market: Some Implications for Human Development', in Cook, P. and Nixson, F. (eds), *The Move to the Market: Trade and Industry Policy Reform in Transitional Economies*, Macmillan.

EPW Research Foundation (1994), 'Social Indicators of Development for India–II, Inter-State Disparities', *Economic and Political Weekly*, 21 May 1994.

Frank, A.G. (1967), *Capitalism and Development in Latin America*, Monthly Review Press.

Franke, R.W. (1993), *Life is a Little Better: Redistribution as a Development Strategy in Nadur Village, Kerala*, Westview Press, Colorado.

Franke, R.W. (1995), 'Is There a Kerala Model?', paper presented at the World Malayalee Convention 1995, July 1–3, Garden State Exhibit Center, Somerset, New Jersey.

Franke, R.W. (1995), 'Kerala State: a Social Justice Model', *Multinational Monitor*, July/August 1995.

Franke, R.W. and Chasin, B. (1990), 'Development without Growth: The Kerala experiment', *Technology Review*, April 1990.

George, K.K. (1990), 'Kerala's Fiscal Crisis: A Diagnosis', *Economic and Political Weekly*, 15 September 1990.

George, K.K. (1993), *Limits to Kerala Model of Development: An Analysis of Fiscal Crisis and Its Implications*, Centre for Development Studies, Thiruvananthapuram, Kerala.

George, K.K. (1994), 'Whither Kerala Model?' paper presented at the International Congress on Kerala Studies at A.K.G. Centre, Thiruvananthapuram, 27–28 August 1994.

George, K.K. (1995), 'Whither Kerala model?', paper presented at the International Congress on Kerala Studies, 27–29 August, 1994, Thiruvananthapuram, Kerala.

George, P.S. (1979), 'Public Distribution of Foodgrains in Kerala – Income Distribution Implications and Effectiveness', Research Report 7, International Food Policy Research Institute, March, 1979.

George, V. (1988), *Wealth, Poverty and Starvation: an International Perspective*, St. Martin Press Inc., New York.

Gopinathan Nair, P.R. (1994), 'Migration of Keralites to the Arab World' in Prakash, B.A. (ed.), *Kerala Economy: Performance, Problems, Prospects*, Sage Publications, New Delhi.

Government of India (1993), *Census of India, Kerala, Series 12, paper 3 of 1991, Final Population Totals*, Samuel, N.M. (ed.).

Government of Kerala (1978), *Women in Kerala*, Bureau of Economics and Statistics, Thiruvananthapuram, Kerala..

Government of Kerala (1984), *Women in Kerala*, Department of Economics and Statistics, Thiruvananthapuram, Kerala.

Government of Kerala (1987), *Evaluation studies: a resume*, Evaluation Division, State Planning Board, Kerala.

Government of Kerala (1989), *Women in Kerala*, Department of Economics and Statistics, Thiruvananthapuram, Kerala.

Government of Kerala (1991), SC/ST devt. spl. cell dept. No. 43/91 dated 12 November 1991.

Government of Kerala (1992), *Kerala at a glance*, Department of Economics and Statistics, Thiruvananthapuram.

Government of Kerala (1992), *Kerala Fisheries: An Overview*, Thiruvananthapuram, Kerala.

Government of Kerala (1994), *Eighth Five Year Plan 1992-97 Mid–Term Review*, State Planning Board, Thiruvananthapuram.

Government of Kerala (1994), *Women in Kerala*, Dept. of Economics and Statistics, Thiruvananthapuram, Kerala.

Government of Kerala (1995), *State Plan of Action for the child in Kerala*.

Government of Kerala, *Economic Review*, various years.

Graff, M.D. (1991), 'Rural Sanitation: A Story of Failures?', *People and Development*, January–February, 1991.

Gulati, I.S. (1995), 'Central funding agencies neglecting Kerala', *The Hindu*, 9 October 1995.

Gulati, I.S. and Gulati, L. (1995), 'Social Security for Widows', *Economic and Political Weekly*, 30 September 1995.

Heller, P. (1995), 'From Class Struggle to Class Compromise: Redistribution and Growth in a South Indian State', *The Journal of Development Studies*, Vol. 31, No. 5, June, 1995.

Hicks, N.L. (1979), 'Growth vs. basic needs: Is there a trade off?', *World Development*, Vol. 7, No. 11/12, 1979.

Hicks, N.L. (1980), Is there a trade off between growth and basic needs?, *Finance and Development*, Vol. 17, No. 2, June 1980.

International Institute for Population Sciences (IIPS), (1995), *National Family Health Survey (MCH and Family Planning), India 1992–93*, Bombay.

Isaac, T.M.T. and Tharakan, P.K.M. (1995), 'Kerala Towards a New Agenda', *Economic and Political Weekly*, 5 August 1995.

James, K.S. (1994), 'Indian Elderly: Asset or Liability', *Economic and Political Weekly*, 3 September 1994.

James, K.S. (1995), 'Transition and Education in Kerala', *Economic and Political Weekly*, 23 December 1995.

Jeffrey, R. (1992), *Politics, Women and Well Being: How Kerala Became a Model*, Delhi: Oxford University Press.

Kannan, K.P. (1990), 'Kerala Economy at the Cross roads?', *Economic and Political Weekly*, 1 September 1990.

Kannan, K.P. (1995), 'Declining Incidence of Rural Poverty in Kerala', *Economic and Political Weekly*, 14 October 1995.

Kannan, K.P., Thankappan, V.R., Ramankutty, V. and Aravindan, K.P. (1991), *Health and Development in Rural Kerala*, Integrated Rural Technology Centre of Kerala Sasthra Sahitya Parishad, Kerala.

Karl, M. (1991), 'Women and Rural Development: an Overview' in ISS Collective (ed.), *Women in Development: a Resource Guide for Organization and Action*, by ISIS Women's International Information and Communication Service, Intermediate Technology Publications.

Kirsty, M. (1995), 'Fertility and Frailty: Demographic Change and Status of Indian Women', *Economic and Political Weekly*, 28 October 1995.

Krishnakumar, (1994), 'Battle against Their Own Minds', *Economic and Political Weekly*, 12 February 1994.

202

Krishnakumar, R. (1996), 'Waiting for their land: tribal people's cause in Kerala', *Frontline*, 13(18):42-43. September 20, 1996.

Krishnaswamy, G. (1998), 'Where poor have access to telephones: Telecommunications and Development in the South Indian State of Kerala', in Mcdonald, S. and Madden, G. (eds), *Telecommunications and Socio-economic Development*, Elsevier Science, North-Holland.

Kumar, R. (1994), 'Development and Women's Work in Kerala: Interactions and Paradoxes', *Economic and Political Weekly*, 17–24 December 1994.

Kumar, S.K. (1979), 'Impact of Subsidized Rice on Food Consumption and Nutrition in Kerala', Research Report 5, International Food Policy Research Institute, January 1979.

Kunhikannan, T.P. and Aravindan, K.P. (1994), 'Pattern of Family Medical Expenditure – a Micro Level Analysis', paper presented at the International Congress on Kerala Studies, 27–29 August 1994, Thiruvananthapuram.

Kurup, K.B. (1991), 'Decentralised Planning for Health and Social Development', *People and Development*, January–February 1991.

Kurup, K.B. (1993), 'Low cost sanitation in India – a historical review', *Kurushetra*, March 1993.

Kurup, K.B. (1994), 'Water, sanitation and health', *Kurushetra*, March 1993.

Kurup, K.B., (1994), 'Water, sanitation and health', *Kurushetra*, March 1994.

Lipton, M. (1995), 'Market, Redistributive and Proto-Reform: Can Liberalization Help the Poor?', *Asian Development Review,* Vol. 13, No. 1.

Longman Active Study Dictionary of English (1991), Longman Group, UK Ltd., England.

MacPherson, S. (1995), 'Social Policy in China in Comparative Perspective' in Wong, L. and MacPherson, S. (eds), *Social Policy and Social Change in China*, Avebury, London.

MacPherson, S. and Lau, K. (1996), 'Measuring Economic and Social Development: Statistical Data on the Pearl River Delta', in MacPherson, S. and Cheng, J.Y.S. (eds), *Economic and Social Development in South China*, Edward Elgar, Aldershot.

Mahadevan, T. and Sumangala, M. (1987), *Social Development, Cultural Change and Fertility Decline: A Study of Fertility Change in Kerala*, Sage, New Delhi.

Mahesh, R. (1994), 'Changing Pattern of Household Consumption in Kerala: Consequences and Opportunities', paper presented at the International Congress on Kerala Studies, 27–29 August 1994, Thiruvananthapuram.

Martin, E. (1979), '... But a Longer Life May Not Be a Better One', *International Development Review*, 1979/1.

McKibben, B. (1995), 'The Enigma of Kerala: One State in India is Proving Development Experts Wrong', *Doubletake*, Summer 1995.

McKibben, B. (1995), *Hope, Human and Wild: True Stories of Living Lightly on Earth*, Brown and Company, Boston, New York, Toronto, London.

McKibben, Bill (1996), 'The enigma of Kerala: one state in India is proving development experts wrong', *Utne Reader*, March-April 1996:103-112.

McNay, K. (1995), 'Fertility and Frailty: Demographic Change and Health and Status of Indian Women', *Economic and Political Weekly*, 28 October 1995.

Monthly Review (1991), Vol. 43, (7) January, 1991.

Morrison, Barrie M. (1997), 'The embourgeoisement of the Kerala farmer', *Modern AsianStudies*,31(1):61-87.

Nag, M. (1983), 'Impact of social and economic development on mortality: Comparative study of Kerala and West Bengal, *Economic and Political Weekly*, Annual Number, 1983.

Nair, P.K.B. (1983), 'Ecology, Social Welfare and Mortality Behaviour: The Case of Kerala, India', *International Review of Sociology*, April–December 1983.

Namboodiripad, E.M.S. (1995), 'Kerala model is one of deindustrialisation', *The Hindu*, 11 September 1995.

Nandamohan, V. (1994), 'Recent Trends in the Industrial Growth of Kerala' in Prakash, B.A. (ed.), *Kerala's economy: Performance, Prospects and Problems*, Sage Publications, New Delhi.

Netherland Television Trust for the Environment (1990), 'Declining Birthrate: Lessons from Kerala' (videorecording).

New Internationalist (1993), No. 241, March 1993.

New Internationalist (1993), Paradox in Paradise: Kerala: India's Radical Success: Special Issue on Kerala, No. 241, 1993.

Nossiter, T.J. (1982), *Communism in Kerala: A Study in Political Adaptation*, C. Hurst and Company, London.

Panikar, P.G.K. and Soman, C.R. (1984), 'Health Status of Kerala: Paradox of Economic Backwardness and Health Development', Centre for Development Studies, Thiruvananthapuram, Kerala.

Parvathamma C. (1986), 'Role of Protest Movements in Social Transformation', *Guru Nanak Journal of Sociology*, April 1986.

Patnaik, P. (1991), 'Four Comments on Kerala', *Monthly Review*, January 1991.

Peterson, W. and Petersen, R. (1986), *Dictionary of Demography – Terms, Concepts, and Institutions*, Greenwood Press, New York.

Prakash, B.A. (1994), 'Kerala Economy: An Overview', in Prakash, B.A. (ed.), *Kerala's Economy: Performance, Problems, Prospects*, Sage Publications, New Delhi.

Radhakrishnan, M.G. (1994), 'Autumn of the Matriarch', *India Today*, 15 December 1994.

Radhakrishnan, M.G. (1996), 'Kerala: Mission Unsuccessful', *India Today*, 15 September 1996.

Radhakrishnan, P. and Akila, R. (1993), 'India's Educational Efforts: Rhetoric and Reality', *Economic and Political Weekly*, 27 November 1993.

Raj, K.N. (1994), 'Has there been a "Kerala model"?', International Congress on Kerala Studies, 27–29 August 1994.

Rajan, S. Irudaya, and V.S. Mishra (1997), 'Restructuring welfare programmes: emerging trends', *Economic and Political Weekly*, 32(6):261-263, February 8, 1997.

Rajmohanan (1994), 'Vaccine Preventable Disease: Situation Analysis and Programme Impication in Kerala', paper presented at the International Congress on Kerala Studies, 27–29 August 1994.

Ram Mohan, K.T. (1991), 'Understanding Keralam: The Tragedy of Radical Scholarship', *Monthly Review*, December, 1991.

Ram, R. (1985), 'The Role of Real Income Level and Income Distribution in Fulfilment of Basic Needs', *World Development*, Vol. 13, No. 5, 1985.

Ramachandran, V.K. (1995), 'A note on Kerala's Development Achievements', *Monthly Review*, May, 1995.

Ramankutty, V. (1993), *Health of Keralites*, Kerala Sastra Sahithya Parishad, Calicut, Kerala.

Reddy, K.N. and Selvaraju, V. (1994), *Health Care Expenditure by Government in India: 1974–75 to 1990–91: Growth, Structure and Priorities by Programme and by Sector*, Seven Hills Publications, New Delhi.

Sadanandan, R. (1993), *The role of Government in the Development of the Health care system in Kerala*, Unpublished M.Phil Dissertation submitted to the Jawaharlal Nehru University.

Saradamoni, K. (1994), 'Women, Kerala and Some Development Issues', *Economic and Political Weekly*, 26 February 1994.

Saradamoni, K. (1995), 'Kerala Mathrukayum Sthreekalum' (Women and Kerala Model) article in Malayalam, *Kerala Padanangal (Kerala Studies)*, Vol. 2.

Satya, P. (1993), 'Unemployment in India: Temporal and Regional Variations', *Economic and Political Weekly*, 30 October 1993.

Seabrook, J. (1993), *Victims of Development: Resistance and Alternatives*, Verso, London and New York.

Seers, D. (1969), 'The Meaning of Development', in Lehmann, D. (ed.), *Development theory: four critical studies*, Cass, London, 1979.

Seers, D. (1977), 'The Meaning of Development: with a Postscript' in Lehmann, David (1979), *Development Theory: Four Critical Studies*, Frank Cass and Company Ltd., London.

Seers, D. (1977), 'The New Meaning of Development', in Lehmann, D. (ed.), *Development Theory: Four Critical Studies*, Cass, London, 1979.

Sen, A. (1993), 'The Economics of Life and Death', *Scientific American*, May 1993.

Sen, A. (1994), 'Population: Delusion and Reality', *The New York Review*, Vol. XLI, No. 15, 22 September 1994.

Sen, A. (1994), 'The Economics of Life and Death', *The New York Review*, May 1993.

Shah, C.H. (1983), 'Food preference, Poverty and the Nutrition Gap', *Economic Development and Cultural Change*, October 1983.

Shiva, V., 'Environmental Impact of Economic Globalization', *Manorama Year Book 1996*, Malayala Manorama, Kottayam, Kerala.

Sidharthan, S., Sukumar, B., Sukumar, A., Neelakantan, V.N., Sreenivasan, A., Ramachandran, M., Jayapal, G., Badaruddin, A., Kumaresan, S., Venugopal, M.G., Mohanan, S., Ajithkumar, M. (1995), *Creation of a Socio-economic Data Base with People's Participation for the Planned Development of Panchayats*, unpublished document.

Singh, M.K. (1981), 'Women and Crime Phenomenon', *The Indian Journal of Social Work*, October 1981.

Sreekumar, T.T. (1993), *Urban process in Kerala*, Centre for Development Studies, Thiruvananthapuram.

Streeten, P. (1972), 'A New Look At Foreign Aid', in Byres, T.J. (ed.), *Foreign Resources and Economic Development*, Frank Cass, London.

Streeten, P. (1981), *First Things First*, London: Oxford University Press, 1981.

Suresh Babu, P. (1995), 'Women are left alone in family welfare', *Janapatham*, November 1995.

Suresh, V. (1991), 'Dispossessed – for Idlis and Dosas!', *The Hindu*, 3 March 1991.

Thankappan, K.R., Kannan, K.P., Ramankutty, V., Aravindan, K.P., Iqbal, B., Kunjikkannan, T.P., Prabhakaran, T.T., Aravindan, S., Asokan, K., Bhaskara Menon, K., Rajiv, V.M., Peethambaran, V., Nandan, P.V., Sasi, V. (1991), *The Health Status of Kerala – A Study*, (Malayalam), Integrated Rural Technology Centre of Kerala Sasthra Sahitya Parishad, Kerala.

The Hindu Online, 'Rethinking Kerala Model', Staff Reporter, 4 August 1996.

The World Bank (1996), *From Plan To Market, World Development Report 1996*, Oxford University Press.

Thomas Isaac, T.M., and K. N. Harilal (1997), 'Planning for empowerment: people's campaign for decentralised planning in Kerala', *Economic and Political Weekly*, 32(1-2):53-58.

Thomas Isaac, T.M., Richard W. Franke, and M. P. Parameswaran (1997), 'From antifeudalism to sustainable development: the Kerala People's Science Movement', *Bulletin of Concerned Asian Scholars*, 29(3):34-44, July-September, 1997.

206

Thomas Isaac, T.M., Richard W. Franke, and Pyaralal Raghavan (1998), *Democracy at Work: The Story of Kerala Dinesh Beedi*. Ithaca, N.Y.: Cornell University Press.

Thomas, A. and Potter, D. (1992), 'Development, Capitalism and the Nation State' in Allen, T. and Thomas, A. (eds), *Poverty and Development in the 1990s*, Oxford, United Kingdom.

Tilak, J.B.G. (1995), *Cost and Financing of Education in India: A Review of Issues, Problems and Prospects*, UNDP Research Project, Centre for Development Studies, Thiruvananthapuram.

Tilak, J.B.G. (1996), 'How Free is 'Free' Primary Education in India? *Economic and Political Weekly*, 3 February 1996.

Timberg, T. (1981), 'Regions in Indian Development', *Pacific Affairs*, Winter, 1980–81.

Time, 'Special Report: Transforming India', 25 March 1996.

UNDP (1993), *Human Development Report*, N.Y., Oxford University Press.

UNDP (1996), *Human Development Report*, N.Y., Oxford University Press.

UNICEF (1995), *The State of the World's Children*, Oxford: Oxford University Press for UNICEF.

UNICEF (1996), 'National Performance Gaps: The Progress of Nations', World Wide Web.

United Nations (1962), *The UN Development Decade: Proposals for Action*, New York: UN.

United Nations (1975), *Poverty, Unemployment and Development Policy: a Case Study of Selected Issues with Reference to Kerala*, New York: United Nations Department of Economic and Social Affairs, Document ST/ESA/29.

Unnithan, N. Prabha (1998), 'Nayars: tradition and change in marriage and fertility', in Womack, Mari (1998), *Being Human: An Introduction to Cultural Anthropology*, Upper Saddle River, New Jersey: Prentice Hall, pp. 348-354.

Vasudevan Nair, P.K. (1995), 'Kerala Model needs follow up', *The Hindu*, 18 September 1995.

Velayudhan, Meera (1998), 'Reform, law and gendered identity: marriage among Ezhavas of Kerala', *Economic and Political Weekly*, 33 (38):2480-83.

Vijayan, Abraham (1998), 'Caste, Class and Agrarian Relations in Kerala', Reliance Publishing House, New Delhi.

Vijayanand (1995), 'Basic Needs Approach in Kerala', unpublished paper.

Wagener, J.H. (1991), Pragmatic and organic change of socio-economic institutions in Dallago, B., Brezinski, H. and Andreff, W. (eds), *Convergence and System Change*, Dartmouth, Aldershot.

WHO (1995), *The World Health Report 1995: Bridging the gaps*, Geneva, Switzerland.

World Bank (1995), *India Country Economic Memorandum: Recent Economic Developments: Achievements and Challenges*, Country Operations, Industry and Finance Division, Country Department II, South Asia Region.

Zachariah, M. and Sooryamoorthy, R. (1994), *Science for Social Revolution: Achievements and Dilemmas of a Development Movement – The Kerala Sastra Sahitya Parishad*, Zed Books, London.

Zachariah, S. et. al (1994), *Demographic Transition in Kerala in the 1980s*, Centre for Development Studies, Trivandrum, Monograph Series.

Index

For Product Safety Concerns and Information please contact our EU representative GPSR@taylorandfrancis.com Taylor & Francis Verlag GmbH, Kaufingerstraße 24, 80331 München, Germany

Printed and bound by CPI Group (UK) Ltd, Croydon, CR0 4YY

08/05/2025

01864394-0002